MGM
Posters

MGM Posters

THE GOLDEN YEARS

TEXT BY FRANK MILLER

JG
PRESS

Published in the USA 1998 by JG Press, Inc
Distributed by World Publications, Inc

The JG Press Imprint is a Trademark of
JG Press, Inc
455 Somerset Avenue
North Dighton, MA 02764

10 9 8 7 6 5 4 3 2

ISBN 1-57215-269-9

Walton Rawls, Vice President, Editorial

Zodie Spain, Editor

Lauren Emerson, Copy Chief

Woolsey Richard Ackerman, Poster Research

Karen E. Smith, Book and Cover Design

Michael Walsh, Vice President, Design

Anne Murdoch, Production Manager

Color separations, film preparation, and printing by Amilcare Pizzi, S. p. A.

Printed in the U.S.A.

OVERLEAF: Campaign art featuring MGM's mascot and trademark, Leo the Lion. Leo was the creation of publicity man Howard Dietz, who would stay with the studio from its birth in 1924 until his retirement in 1957. The lion first roared in 1921, when Dietz designed it as the logo for Goldwyn Pictures.

Table of Contents

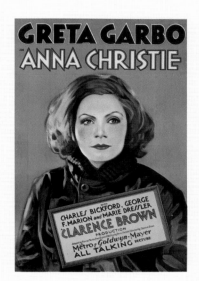

Introduction

The Girl of the Golden West

(1938) PROMOTIONAL ART

THE GIRL OF THE GOLDEN WEST (1938): In 1938, audiences tired of the Depression and political unrest in Europe could lose themselves in the wide-open spaces as Jeanette MacDonald and Nelson Eddy sang their way through *The Girl of the Golden West*. (Opposite) A member of MGM's publicity department prepares a poster concept for *The Girl of the Golden West* (1938). Note the production stills used as models and the finished posters on the wall. The 24 sheet *Conquest* poster is on page 47.

REAMS FOR SALE! That's what Hollywood had to offer an eager world during the days of the great movie studios. From the construction of the first Hollywood backlot in 1908 through the decline of the studio system in the fifties and sixties, legendary production companies like Warner Bros., RKO, Paramount, and Universal fed devoted audiences glamorized visions of their most cherished hopes, sanitized versions of their darkest fears. ✳ Dream-making was big business, and like any business, Hollywood depended on advertising to make its product, its dreams, an essential part of people's lives. Nobody did this better than MGM. Within two years of the company's creation in 1924, MGM led the industry in the quality and popularity of its movies. It also set the pace in advertising, spending $1.5 million a year in the twenties and more than $3 million a year by the late thirties. ✳ MGM's advertising, under the direction of West Coast publicity chief Howard Strickling, was as classy as the films it sold, thanks largely to the work of two men, publicity director Howard Dietz and art director Hal Burrows. Dietz was one of several key personnel the company inherited during the mergers that created MGM. He originally worked for Goldwyn Pictures, where he created the lion's head logo that would become MGM's trademark. Among his many talents was a facility for language, for not only did he write such great MGM slogans as "More Stars Than There Are in Heaven," but he crafted the lyrics to dozens of hit Broadway musicals. ✳ Burrows tapped the cream of American illustrators—Al Hirschfeld, Alberto Vargas, Armando Seguso, Jacques Kapralik, and William Galbraith Crawford, among many others—to help create some of the industry's best posters. He supervised a simple, uncluttered design style that drew attention to MGM's top assets: its stars. ✳ MGM maintained only a small staff to supervise the creation of advertising art, never employing more than eight people at a time. As soon as a story was approved, images were shot by one of the studio's still photographers. From these, Dietz and Burrows created poster concepts to be sent out to free-lance artists. They trusted their artists and gave them unprecedented freedom to develop new concepts, but also typed them very carefully, exploiting each one's greatest strengths. Future Broadway caricaturist Hirschfeld was assigned primarily to comedies and musicals. John Held Jr., who had achieved fame illustrating F. Scott Fitzgerald's stories, also concentrated on comedies, specializing in jazz-age stories. Ted Ireland, who signed his work "Vincentini," was best at glamor portraits of the stars; Hirschfeld would later dub him MGM's "eye, ears, nose and throat specialist." ✳ Artists usually

When *Meet Me in St. Louis* premiered at the Astor theater in November 1944, it was such a huge hit that it moved directly across the street to Loew's State as soon as its booking was finished. These were the last days of vaudeville, when live stage shows alternated between movie screenings, and often the marquee and poster windows shared announcement space. Among the poster art that Loew's State displayed were marquee banners and a three sheet (seen on right side poster window).

completed an assignment in one or two days. The pay was low—rarely more than $35–50 per design. Most work was unsigned, and the artist had to eliminate any stylistic elements that might be too distinctive. Frequently, a single design would be used in a variety of media or even recycled for other films. But most of the artists loved the freedom Dietz gave them and the prestige of working for Hollywood's top studio. ✳ Advertising art reached the audience in a variety of formats:

- One sheets: Single sheet posters, usually 27 inches by 41 inches, mounted in display cases at the front of the theater. One sheets come in different styles, usually two to four per film.
- Three sheets: Although they come in two pieces, three sheets derive their name from the fact that they are three times the length of one sheets, measuring 81 inches by 41 inches. Typically there are two styles available per film.
- Six sheets: Six times the size of a one sheet, measuring 81 inches by 82 inches, these were used for small billboards.
- Twenty-four sheets: Used for larger billboards.
- Half-sheets: 22 inches by 28 inches.
- Inserts: 14 inches by 36 inches.

- Lobby Cards: Sets of eight 11" x 14" cards displayed in theater lobbies. Each complete set contains a title card listing cast and other credits as well as seven scene cards, each hand colored.
- Campaign Books: Promotional tools sent to potential exhibitors. Campaign books include biographies, publicity articles, newspaper quotes, information for radio announcements, cast and credits, ads, propaganda displays, articles, games, merchandising, theater accessories, and posters. Most of the available poster styles for a film are displayed on the back of the campaign book.

✳ Although MGM valued the role of posters in selling a movie, as artwork they bore no great value. Theaters paid as little as $.35 each for posters, which were often eventually thrown into storage closets, or simply junked. Fans who asked for posters often got them for free. Even as recently as 1965, an original poster for *The Wizard of Oz* could be bought for as little as $15. ✳ Gradually, however, poster collecting became a big business. In 1993, a *Red Headed Woman* one sheet sold at auction for $9,800, while a *Wizard of Oz* half-sheet

The Wizard of Oz
(1939) CAMPAIGN BOOK BACK

Among the many items included in a campaign book was a presentation of much of the poster art available for theater owners to order. The large size posters were displayed in full color on the backs of the campaign books. MGM employed its various advertising artists to come up with the extremely varied array of poster concepts for the film. Al Hirschfeld, whose work is seen on the six sheet, three sheet B, jumbo window card and one sheets C and D, was one of the contributors.

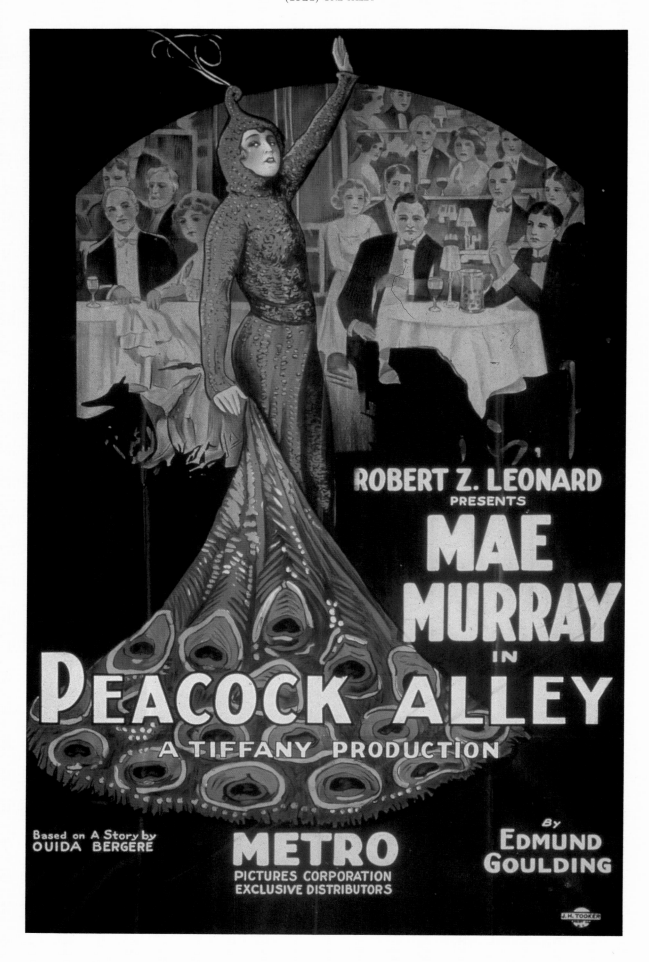

PEACOCK ALLEY (1921): Mae Murray, "The Girl With the Bee-Stung Lips," was one of several stars Louis B. Mayer inherited with the formation of MGM. Some of Murray's best pictures were made under the direction of her third husband, Robert Z. Leonard, who would become one of MGM's most successful and prolific directors.

THE FOUR HORSEMEN OF THE APOCALYPSE (1921): Metro Pictures had its first hit with this lavish film about the effect of World War I on a wealthy Argentine family. The picture made Rudolph Valentino a star, made Rex Ingram one of Metro's, and later MGM's, hottest directors of the day and provided MGM with several lucrative reissues.

went for $10,000. The most valuable posters feature the most famous films or the biggest stars. A *King Kong* three sheet was auctioned for more than $100,000 in 1991. Experts predict that before the century's end, the most coveted posters will sell for $250,000 or more, drawing the same bids as many great works of art. ❋ The rarity of vintage movie posters helps account for their growing value, but there's more to it than that. Movie art, particularly from Hollywood's golden age, provides a passport to simpler times, when the movies expressed basic dreams shared by large numbers of Americans. They also open a window on history, tracing changes in American life as reflected in popular entertainment and the growth of film as both business and art form. ❋ The posters collected in this book reflect a more specialized view of film history. Starting with the first official MGM production, 1924's *He Who Gets Slapped*, they tell the story of Hollywood's greatest studio from its creation to its rise to industry leader to the end of the studio system. Along the way, they depict the rise and fall of some of the screen's greatest stars, and the growth and decline of such popular genres as the musical and the horror film. They also capture memories of some of MGM's greatest movies, placed in perspective against the studio's own great history. ❋ So here they are, the masterpieces and the time-passers; the enduring stars and the one-shot wonders; the hits, the flops, and the bread-and-butter pictures that kept things running. As you travel through these pages, you'll discover the history of an American institution—MGM—as told through the images the studio used to sell its dreams to the world.

The Twenties

OLLYWOOD'S GREATEST DREAM factory was a child of economic necessity. Like many exhibitors in the teens and twenties, Marcus Loew wanted to move into production to guarantee his theaters a steady supply of high-quality product. At the same time, Metro Pictures, which had been founded in 1915, wanted to expand into exhibition to provide a guaranteed market for its product. ✳ In 1921, the two entities merged, with Loews, Inc., as parent company. When Loew realized that he needed more product than Metro could supply, he bought the ailing Goldwyn Studios (two years after the departure of founder Sam Goldwyn), complete with its lion trademark and lavish backlot in Culver City, California. A manager was needed for the new operation so a fourth entity was added to the mix: Louis B. Mayer. ✳ Mayer had been producing films for five years and had just acquired the services of a twenty-four-year-old production executive already being touted as Hollywood's "boy wonder," Irving G. Thalberg. Within two years, they would make the newly created MGM studios Hollywood's most profitable production company. ✳ Mayer knew the wisdom of building a solid stable of contract talent and set out to make MGM the studio with "more stars than the heavens." As head of his own company, he had acquired the services of Lon Chaney and Norma Shearer. From Metro came Ramon Novarro and Buster Keaton, while Goldwyn Pictures brought him Mae Murray and John Gilbert. Within a few years, Mayer would add some of MGM's biggest stars, including Greta Garbo, Lillian Gish, and one-time chorus girl Lucille Le Sueur, who would be redubbed Joan Crawford in a studio contest. ✳ The first film planned and produced by MGM was *He Who Gets Slapped,* starring Lon Chaney, but the picture that put the new studio on the map was a troubled production started at Goldwyn, the 1925 *Ben-Hur.* That same year, MGM would have its first mega-hit with *The Big Parade,* the screen's first serious look back at World War I. Thalberg also demonstrated a surprising willingness to take artistic risks when he backed two commercially questionable projects for director King Vidor: the slice-of-life drama *The Crowd,* a film Mayer loathed, and the all-black musical *Hallelujah.* ✳ Hit would follow hit for the new studio, but as the decade ended, MGM and the rest of Hollywood would face a new crisis—the advent of sound. Talking pictures, a boon at the box office, helped Hollywood weather increased competition from radio and the disastrous effects of the Depression, but they were also a threat as old filmmaking techniques—and old stars—had to adapt or fall in the face of the new medium.

HE WHO GETS SLAPPED (1924): The first film produced entirely under the MGM aegis set a high standard the studio would match repeatedly. Three major stars—Lon Chaney, John Gilbert, and the up-and-coming Norma Shearer—joined forces for this poetic adaptation of Russian-born Leonid Andreyev's acclaimed play.

He Who Gets Slapped

(1924) ONE SHEET
ILLUSTRATOR: ALVIN WOLFSON

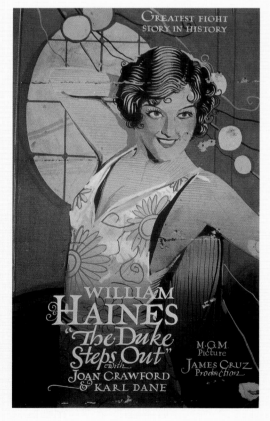

The Duke Steps Out

(1929) ONE SHEET
ILLUSTRATOR: RUSSELL ROBERTS

Our Modern Maidens

(1929) THREE SHEET

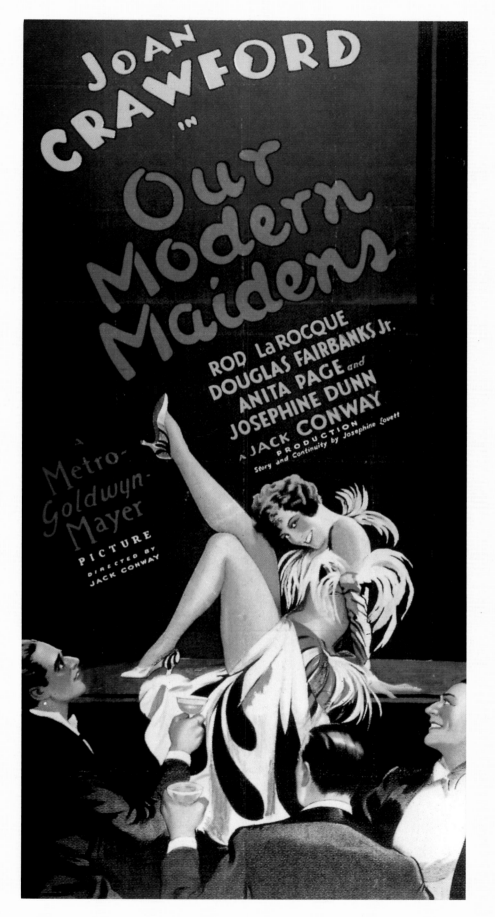

SPITE MARRIAGE (1929): After Buster Keaton signed a new contract with MGM in 1928, Mayer and production chief Irving G. Thalberg kept him out of talking pictures as long as possible. This underrated 1929 comedy was both his second MGM feature and his last silent film.

THE DUKE STEPS OUT (1929): Joan Crawford was one of the first big stars developed at MGM. As with many a young player, the studio paired her with established stars like athletic comic William Haines, her co-star in *The Duke Steps Out*. Although changing styles and off-screen scandal would end Haines's career in the early thirties, he and Crawford would remain close friends for life.

OUR MODERN MAIDENS (1929): As the wild-living flapper in *Our Dancing Daughters*, Crawford had shot to stardom in 1928. MGM reteamed her with co-stars Anita Page and Dorothy Sebastian for two similar tales of flaming youth, *Our Modern Maidens* (1929) and *Our Blushing Brides* (1930).

THE BIG PARADE (1925): Irving G. Thalberg got the production go-ahead on Hollywood's first big World War I epic over Louis B. Mayer's objections. When the King Vidor film became a hit, making John Gilbert the studio's number-one star, this triggered a rift between Mayer and Thalberg that would continue until the latter's death.

BARDELYS THE MAGNIFICENT (1926): With the success of *The Big Parade*, Gilbert and Vidor reteamed for *La Boheme* (1926) and this lavish swashbuckler based on a Rafael Sabatini novel. Gilbert was rushed into the film after he turned down the chance to team with Greta Garbo in her second film, *The Temptress* (1926).

Bardelys the Magnificent

(1926) ART COMMISSIONED FOR EASTMAN THEATER
ILLUSTRATOR: BATISTE MADALENA

The Student Prince in Old Heidelberg

(1927) Art commissioned for Eastman Theater
Illustrator: Batiste Madalena

Faust

(1926) insert

So This is College

(1929) one sheet
Illustrator: John Held Jr.

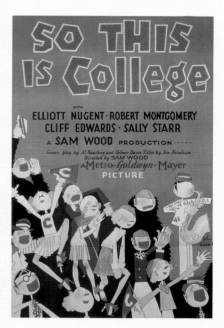

BEN-HUR (1925): The film that put MGM on the map was actually a Goldwyn picture already in production when Louis B. Mayer took over. Mayer shut down the beleaguered shoot and replaced director Charles Brabin and leading man George Walsh with Fred Niblo and Ramon Novarro, respectively. The result was a spectacular triumph, but production expenses and Goldwyn's costly deal for the rights to Lew Wallace's novel kept the film in the red for years.

FAUST (1926): MGM frequently picked up domestic distribution rights to European films like F. W. Murnau's German classic *Faust*, starring Emil Jannings as the devil. Both Murnau and Jannings would soon travel to Hollywood. The coming of sound would end the heavily accented actor's career, while Murnau would die in an automobile accident at the age of forty-two.

THE STUDENT PRINCE IN OLD HEIDELBERG (1927): MGM showcased rising stars Norma Shearer and Ramon Novarro in this lavish silent version of the Sigmund Romberg operetta. Novarro took top billing on the strength of his work in *Ben-Hur,* but the month the film opened, Shearer cemented her own MGM stardom by marrying the boss, Irving G. Thalberg.

SO THIS IS COLLEGE (1929): After making his film debut in *Three Live Ghosts* at United Artists, Robert Montgomery moved to MGM for this college musical—and stayed for seventeen years. Through most of his career, Montgomery would play sleek high-society types like his character in this picture.

The Scarlet Letter

(1926) WINDOW CARD

Laugh Clown Laugh

(1927) ONE SHEET

THE SCARLET LETTER (1926): Lillian Gish brought so much prestige to MGM when she signed on in 1925 that Mayer gave her unparalled artistic control. Her first two films, *La Boheme* (1926) and this adaptation of Nathaniel Hawthorne's classic, were both critical and box-office successes.

THE WIND (1928): Lillian Gish had a critical success with this tale of a young girl driven mad in the Wild West, but the picture was a box-office disaster. Both studio and star agreed to cut Gish's contract short after only five films.

LAUGH CLOWN LAUGH (1927): With Lon Chaney's success in *He Who Gets Slapped*, it was only natural he should play a clown again. In this adaptation of David Belasco's stage play, the fifteen-year-old Loretta Young made her MGM debut as the object of Chaney's unrequited love.

THE UNKNOWN (1927): Lon Chaney, "The Man of a Thousand Faces," dazzled audiences as an armless man using his feet as substitute hands, while Joan Crawford co-starred as the young woman he loves.

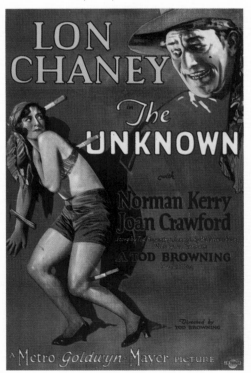

The Unknown

(1927) ONE SHEET

LONDON AFTER MIDNIGHT (1927): Shots of Chaney in his dual role as a vampire and a Scotland Yard investigator are almost all that remain of this lost horror classic, written and directed by Tod Browning.

THE BLACK BIRD (1925): Audiences loved films that capitalized on Chaney's versatility and his ability to contort his body. In this thriller, his second film with Browning, he starred as a thief who masquerades as a mission worker with twisted legs.

THE UNHOLY THREE (1925): Browning had directed Chaney in two lesser films at other studios, but the team hit paydirt when Chaney begged MGM to put them together for this tale of a trio of sideshow cons running a crime ring. They would go on to make seven other films together and were planning another when Chaney died.

London After Midnight

(1927) TITLE LOBBY CARD

The Black Bird

(1925) ART COMMISSIONED FOR EASTMAN THEATER
ILLUSTRATOR: BATISTE MADALENA

The Broadway Melody
(1929) ART FOR ONE SHEET
ILLUSTRATORS: AL HIRSCHFELD AND WILLIAM GALBRAITH CRAWFORD

THE BROADWAY MELODY (1929): MGM marked the end of one era and the birth of another with the release of the studio's first all-talking feature. Although the back-stage musical seems seriously dated now, it was such a breakthrough in its day that it brought MGM its first Oscar for Best Picture.

HALLELUJAH (1929): Director King Vidor was so fervent in his desire to make Hollywood's first feature with an all-black cast that he offered to work without a salary. Mayer only approved the project because he was busy working on Herbert Hoover's presidential campaign.

(1929) ART FOR ONE SHEET
ILLUSTRATOR: AL HIRSCHFELD

GREED (1924): Erich von Stroheim's masterpiece was originally a Goldwyn picture and had been sitting on the shelf for a year when MGM was formed. Thalberg cut the seven-hour epic to just over ninety minutes, a loss film critics have mourned for decades.

THE MERRY WIDOW (1925): Despite their differences, Thalberg respected von Stroheim's talent enough to hire him for MGM's lavish film version of Franz Lehar's classic operetta. Problems on the set (star Mae Murray referred to von Stroheim as "that dirty Hun") would make this the last film he would direct at MGM.

FLESH AND THE DEVIL (1926): John Gilbert turned down the chance to co-star with Greta Garbo in *The Temptress*, but working together at last, the two stars reportedly kept their love scenes going long after director Clarence Brown yelled cut.

Greed
(1924) LOBBY CARD

The Merry Widow
(1925) TITLE LOBBY CARD

The Single Standard
(1929) ONE SHEET

The Mysterious Lady
(1928) ONE SHEET

A Woman of Affairs
(1928) ONE SHEET
ILLUSTRATOR: WILLIAM GALBRAITH CRAWFORD

THE SINGLE STANDARD (1929): Garbo continued her reign as the screen's most provocative star with this Adela Rogers St. John tale of a free spirit out to prove that women could be just as promiscuous as men.

THE MYSTERIOUS LADY (1928): Until her emergence as a superstar in the thirties, Garbo made her share of potboilers, including this improbable spy tale.

A WOMAN OF AFFAIRS (1928): Things had changed by the time Garbo and Gilbert made their third film together. This time, she had top billing, at least on screen.

THE KISS (1929): With the coming of sound ending the careers of other heavily accented European stars, MGM vowed to keep Garbo speechless as long as possible. This courtroom drama was Garbo's—and the studio's—last silent film.

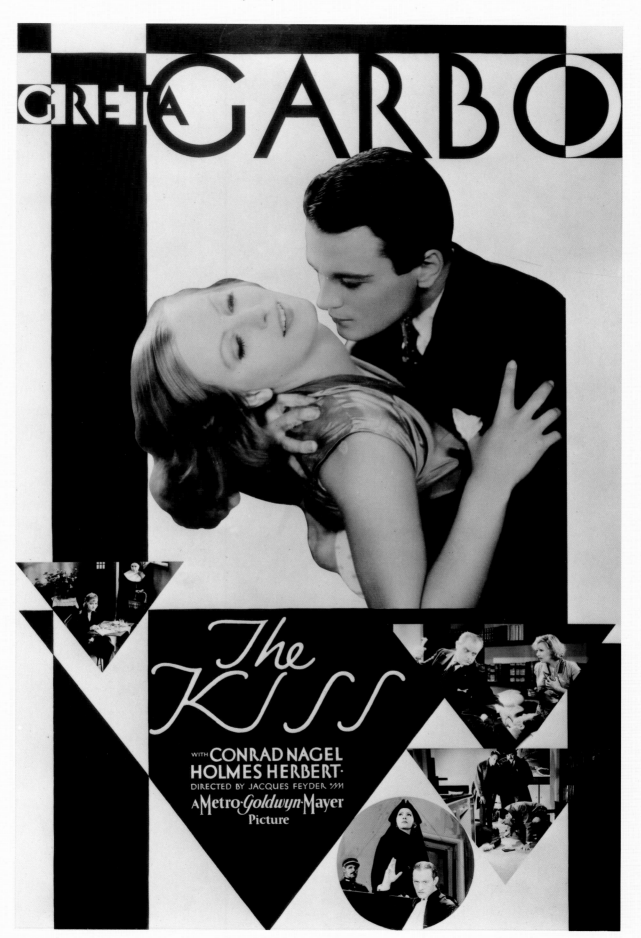

The Thirties

MGM SURVIVED THE COMING of sound to continue its reign as Hollywood's top studio. Greta Garbo emerged as a bigger star than ever after her talking film debut. Also growing in stature were Norma Shearer and Joan Crawford. The studio's main casualty to sound was John Gilbert. ✻ New stars would soon rise to the top at MGM. Eleanor Powell, Nelson Eddy, and Jeanette MacDonald dominated the talking era's new sensation, the musical. Jean Harlow, Clark Gable, Myrna Loy, Spencer Tracy, William Powell, and James Stewart excelled in nonsinging roles. And Judy Garland and Mickey Rooney became the studio's top juvenile stars. ✻ Thalberg shepherded hit after hit through MGM's production line, helped tremendously by such producers as Joseph L. Mankiewicz and Walter Wanger. In addition, Mayer convinced his son-in-law, David O. Selznick, to put in a few years at the studio. ✻ MGM's films took place in a world far removed from the realities of the Depression or the political unrest in Europe. The real world intruded on their make-believe only in 1934, when a church-led campaign against on-screen indecency, coupled with the delayed effects of the Depression, triggered a drop in ticket sales that led to the creation of the Production Code, Hollywood's system of self-censorship from the thirties into the sixties. ✻ To make their stars the most appealing in the world, MGM hired the best designers and technicians in the business. Their work earned MGM the nickname "The House of Glamour," yet the studio's number-one star in the early years of the decade was Marie Dressler, a weather-beaten character actress in her sixties. ✻ The thirties was a decade of technical development for MGM. Norma Shearer's brother, Douglas, helped turn sound recording into an art form. After years of experimenting with a two color photography process, Technicolor developed the more versatile three-strip process used today. ✻ But the thirties were also a decade of loss for the studio. Marie Dressler succumbed to cancer in 1934. Wanger and Selznick both moved into independent production. Worst of all, Thalberg died at the tragically young age of thirty-seven, a loss the studio would feel increasingly through the forties. ✻ As the decade came to a close, the studio's New York money-men were concerned about the war in Europe. The loss of that market led MGM to focus increasingly on all-American stories and personalities to increase domestic ticket sales. Even Garbo switched tactics and starred in her first comedy, 1939's *Ninotchka*. Within a few years, MGM would be thrust into a new world of wartime film production that would make the studio more successful than ever,

ANNA CHRISTIE (1930): Only the best would do for the talking-film debut of MGM's greatest asset, Greta Garbo. When George Bernard Shaw refused to sell the rights to *Saint Joan*, Thalberg chose Eugene O'Neill's *Anna Christie.* Garbo's performance allayed any fears about her speaking voice.

GRAND HOTEL (1932): Star power and studio glamor set the standard for MGM's thirties output. Irving G. Thalberg created the first all-star cast for *Grand Hotel*, winning MGM its second Best Picture Oscar.

DINNER AT EIGHT (1933): A year after *Grand Hotel*, David O. Selznick followed suit with his adaptation of the George S. Kaufman-Edna Ferber stage comedy.

BILLY THE KID (1930): This 1930 Western is noteworthy for presenting the notorious outlaw (played by John Mack Brown) as a misunderstood rebel. Less successful was MGM's attempt to introduce "Realife," a wide-screen process similar to Cinemascope.

THE SON-DAUGHTER (1932): Despite her Oscar-winning performance in *The Sin of Madelon Claudet* (1931), Helen Hayes was never comfortable as an MGM star. Nor did the studio know how to use her talents, as demonstrated by this muddled tale of family feuds in San Francisco's Chinatown.

Dinner at Eight

(1933) TITLE LOBBY CARD
ILLUSTRATOR: WILLIAM GALBRAITH CRAWFORD

The Son-Daughter
(1932) ONE SHEET

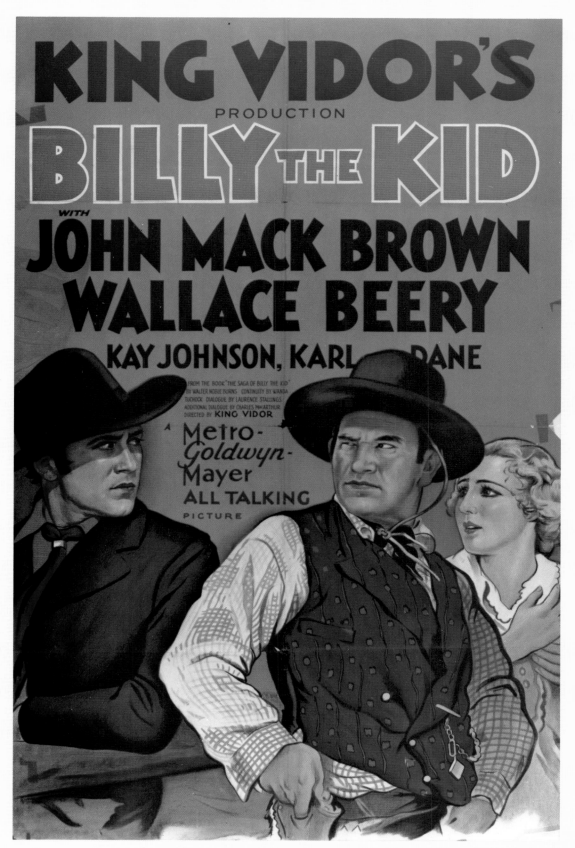

Billy the Kid
(1930) ONE SHEET

Blondie of the Follies
(1932) ONE SHEET

Polly of the Circus
(1932) ONE SHEET

TUGBOAT ANNIE (1933): The house of glamor's number-one leading lady of the thirties was the far from glamorous Marie Dressler, whose talents were perfectly suited to this tale of a female tugboat captain brawling with her husband (Wallace Beery) while sacrificing all for her son (Robert Young).

BLONDIE OF THE FOLLIES (1932): Marion Davies was not a true MGM star. The studio distributed the films produced on the lot by publisher William Randolph Hearst's independent Cosmopolitan Pictures, a deal inherited from Goldwyn Pictures. Davies drew on her background as a Ziegfeld girl for this backstage musical.

POLLY OF THE CIRCUS (1932): Marion Davies's films were expensive—drawing on such top MGM talent as Clark Gable, cast improbably as a minister in love with a beautiful trapeze artist—and tended to lose money. The studio's compensation was favorable treatment in Hearst's newspapers and from his powerful gossip columnist, Louella Parsons.

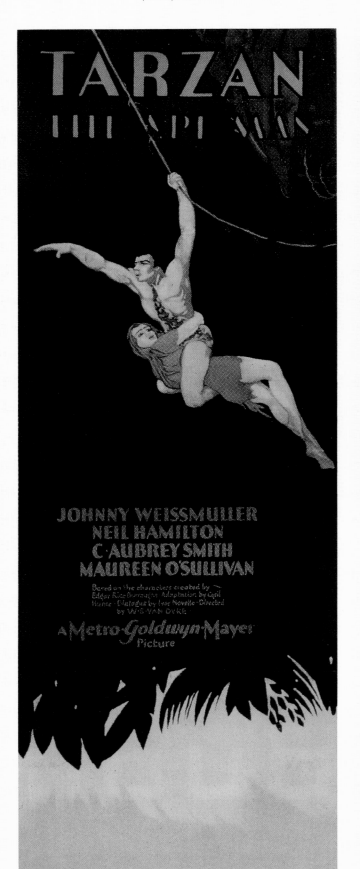

TARZAN THE APE MAN (1932): Johnny Weissmuller beat out thirty-six other contenders—including Clark Gable and Joel McCrea—to star in this lavish production, a far cry from the quickie jungle films churned out by other studios. Helping the film score at the box office was Maureen O'Sullivan's performance as Jane, a perfect blend of innocence, humor, and sex appeal.

TARZAN AND HIS MATE (1934): MGM made audiences wait two years for a Tarzan sequel, but it was worth it; many critics consider this the best of the series. It certainly had the sexiest costumes (though you couldn't tell it from this poster). With the arrival of stricter Hollywood censorship, Tarzan and Jane would have to cover up more in the future.

TARZAN ESCAPES (1936): The third Tarzan film was supposed to be geared more to juvenile audiences, but when it previewed, audiences were shocked by its many grisly sequences, including an attack by giant vampire bats. Mayer ordered the film substantially reshot, a common practice for MGM.

TARZAN FINDS A SON! (1939): Tarzan finished the thirties by adopting an orphaned boy (Johnny Sheffield) lost in the jungle. He had to "find" the child, because of censors' complaints that Tarzan and Jane had never legally married. Originally the film concluded with Jane's death (O'Sullivan wanted out of the series), but shocked fans demanded a new ending.

CONGO MAISIE (1939): Wise-cracking comedienne Ann Sothern inherited the role of showgirl Maisie Ravier when Jean Harlow died. When the first *Maisie* film became a hit, MGM cast her in this sequel, loosely based on one of Harlow's biggest hits, *Red Dust* (1932). John Carroll took over the Gable role.

YOUNG DR. KILDARE (1938): MGM launched another profitable series when Lew Ayres and Lionel Barrymore starred in this adaptation of Max Brand's medical novels. Although the series would last until 1948, Ayres was dropped in 1942, after he registered for the draft as a conscientious objector, and Hollywood temporarily turned against him.

THE MASK OF FU MANCHU (1932): Despite MGM's commitment to family films, the studio went all out with this exercise in sadism and perversion adapted from Sax Rohmer's novels. Boris Karloff, still riding high on the success of *Frankenstein*, may have been the box-office name, but Myrna Loy, in her last Oriental seductress role, took all honors for villainy.

THE UNHOLY 3 (1930): Lon Chaney resisted the move to talking pictures at first, then dazzled audiences by using five different voices for this remake of his silent hit. He was set to star in Universal's *Dracula* when he died of throat cancer just seven weeks after *The Unholy 3*'s premiere.

Congo Maisie
(1939) ONE SHEET

Young Dr. Kildare
(1938) ONE SHEET

The Mask of Fu Manchu
(1932) WINDOW CARD

The Unholy 3
(1930) INSERT

MAD LOVE (1935): After Lon Chaney's death, horror films became a rarity at MGM. With the ongoing success of other studios' fright films, however, MGM imported Peter Lorre to make his U.S. film debut in this strange, poetic tale, based on the French novel *The Hands of Orlac* (the film's title in England).

MARK OF THE VAMPIRE (1935): Tod Browning remade his lost silent, *London After Midnight,* with two actors in the Lon Chaney role: Lionel Barrymore and Bela Lugosi as the vampire.

THE DEVIL DOLL (1936): "We'll make the whole world small!" screamed mad scientist Rafaela Ottiano in this eerie tale of an escaped convict (Lionel Barrymore) who masquerades as an old woman to slip doll-sized killers into his enemies' homes.

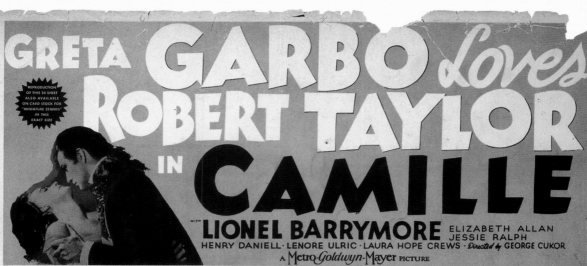

CAMILLE (1936): Many have called Garbo's performance as the doomed courtesan in this adaptation of the Alexandre Dumas, *fils*, play the finest ever recorded on screen. Some fans even claimed that during the star's climactic death scene they saw her soul leave her body.

NINOTCHKA (1939): With the war threatening to cut off the European market, MGM set out to broaden Garbo's appeal at home by putting her in her first comedy. The Billy Wilder-Charles Brackett script gave her the perfect role, a cold-blooded Soviet official warmed up by Paris and diplomat Melvyn Douglas.

THE PAINTED VEIL (1934): This adaptation of W. Somerset Maugham's story seemed a return to the vehicles of Garbo's silent days, casting her as a woman torn between her noble if stodgy husband (Herbert Marshall) and a passionate young man (George Brent).

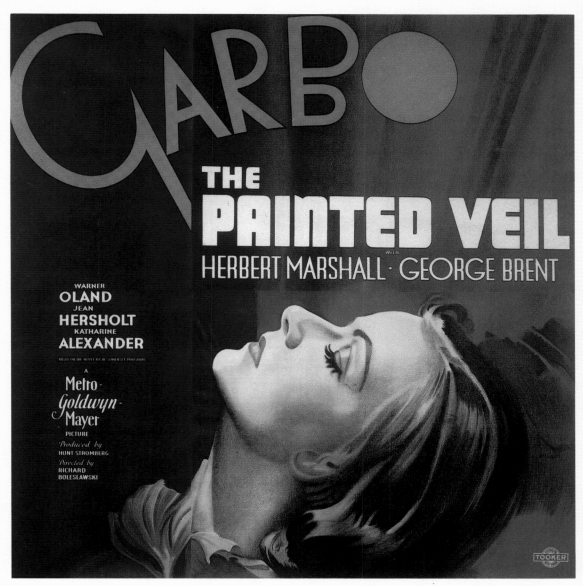

The Painted Veil

(1934) SIX SHEET
ILLUSTRATOR: VINCENTINI

ROMANCE (1930): Garbo's husky speaking voice added to her mystique, making her a bigger star than ever. Here she plays an operatic soprano kept by one man (Lewis Stone) but in love with another (Gavin Gordon).

ANNA KARENINA (1935): Producer David O. Selznick wanted to cast Garbo as the dying heiress in *Dark Victory*, but she insisted on this screen version of Leo Tolstoy's classic novel. She had already starred in a silent version, *Love* (1927), with John Gilbert.

AS YOU DESIRE ME (1932): Thalberg was so sure that Luigi Pirandello's play was a pefect Garbo vehicle that he bought the rights before its Broadway opening. He also buried the hatchet by casting Erich von Stroheim in the male lead.

MATA HARI (1931): Garbo was at her most seductive playing the notorious World War I spy, so much so that censors complained about the revealing outfit depicted on the poster.

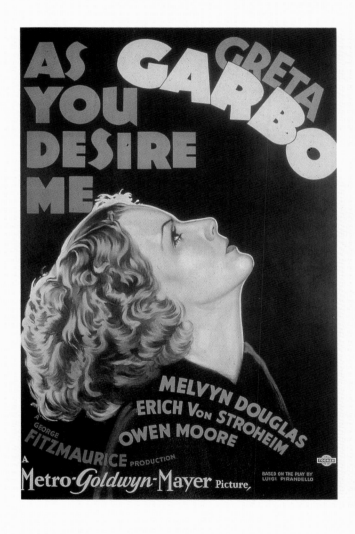

As You Desire Me

(1932) ONE SHEET

Mata Hari

(1931) 1941 REISSUE INSERT

QUEEN CHRISTINA (1934): After almost two years off-screen, Garbo signed a new MGM contract granting her almost total control over her films. She exercised that control by getting leading man Laurence Olivier fired and forcing Mayer to replace him with former co-star and lover John Gilbert, whose career had faltered since the coming of sound.

CONQUEST (1937): After an arduous and costly production schedule, this historical epic was a disappointment. Garbo was overshadowed by co-star Charles Boyer, cast as Napoleon, and the film did poorly domestically, only moving into the black through lucrative international bookings. But the European market was about to dry up with the start of World War II.

A FREE SOUL (1931): Second only to Garbo at MGM was Norma Shearer, the wife of production chief Irving G. Thalberg, but also a star in her own right. Audiences ate it up when Clark Gable manhandled her in the screen version of Adela Rogers St. Johns's autobiographical novel. The film made both bigger stars than ever.

STRANGE INTERLUDE (1932): Thalberg reunited Shearer and Gable for the film version of Eugene O'Neill's Pulitzer Prize-winning play. Nine writers tackled the mammoth psycho-sexual drama in which the actors speak their characters' thoughts. Audiences came to see the stars, but many stayed to snicker.

IDIOT'S DELIGHT (1939): Shearer and Gable looked great in this adaptation of Robert E. Sherwood's antiwar romance, and Gable got to deliver a show-stopping rendition of "Putting on the Ritz."

Strange Interlude

(1932) TITLE LOBBY CARD

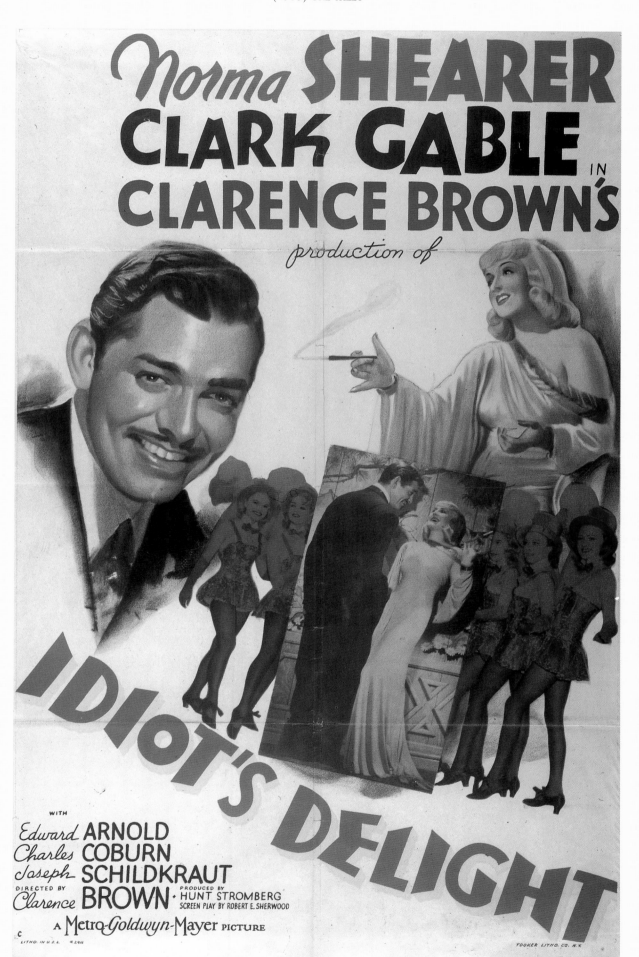

ROMEO AND JULIET (1936): Thalberg lavished more attention on this Shakespearean adaptation than he had on any other film, primarily because he hoped it would establish Shearer as a great actress. Although her careful study of the role impressed the critics, the film lost almost one million dollars, making it Thalberg's biggest box-office failure.

MARIE ANTOINETTE (1938): Before he could start production on Shearer's next epic, Thalberg died at the age of thirty-seven. After a year of mourning, Shearer returned to MGM to fulfill her husband's last dream. The result was a fast-moving, lengthy picture that had some critics gnashing their teeth, but gave Shearer a stunning comeback.

THE BARRETTS OF WIMPOLE STREET (1934): William Randolph Hearst and Marion Davies left MGM when Thalberg beat them out for the rights to this romantic tale about Robert and Elizabeth Barrett Browning. Joining Shearer was fellow Oscar-winner Fredric March and Charles Laughton, who would win his own Academy Award during filming.

The Barretts of Wimpole Street
(1934) INSERT

THOROUGHBREDS DON'T CRY (1937): MGM had a pair of immensely gifted youngsters under contract. This horse-racing story marked Judy Garland's rise to star billing and her first teaming with frequent co-star Mickey Rooney.

LOVE FINDS ANDY HARDY (1938): A year later, Garland moved into Rooney's popular Andy Hardy series with a semiregular role as singing heiress Betsy Booth. Making her studio debut was Lana Turner.

JUDGE HARDY AND SON (1939): Of all the MGM series, the Andy Hardy films were the most popular and the dearest to Mayer's heart. Mayer even wrote one of Mickey Rooney's speeches for this, the eighth Hardy film.

BABES IN ARMS (1939): Garland and Rooney kicked off a series of "Putting on a Show" teen musicals with this adaptation of the Richard Rodgers-Lorenz Hart stage hit. The picture also marked the first producing credit for Arthur Freed, the one-time songwriter who would give MGM some of its greatest musicals.

Love Finds Andy Hardy
(1938) ONE SHEET

Babes in Arms
(1939) THREE SHEET

Judge Hardy and Son
(1939) ONE SHEET

The Merry Widow
(1934) ONE SHEET

BORN TO DANCE (1936): As Mayer and Thalberg built up the studio's star roster, they assembled an impressive array of musical talent, including Eleanor Powell, the greatest tap-dancing lady of them all. They even tried to make James Stewart into a musical star for this feature, in which he introduced Cole Porter's "Easy to Love."

THE MERRY WIDOW (1934): Jeanette MacDonald became a major MGM star after being rushed in to replace opera-singer Grace Moore in this re-make of the studio's silent hit. Co-star Maurice Chevalier had not liked work-ing with MacDonald in such Paramount films as *Love Me Tonight*, but main-tained his Gallic charm throughout.

THE FIREFLY (1937): MacDonald was perfectly capable of carrying a film on her own, as she did with this adaptation of Rudolf Friml's operetta about a Spanish spy working against Napoleon. It was co-star Allan Jones, however, who sang the film's biggest hit, "The Donkey Serenade."

The Firefly
(1937) ONE SHEET

NAUGHTY MARIETTA (1935): MGM made history by teaming MacDonald with Nelson Eddy for this Victor Herbert tunefest.

ROSE MARIE (1936): For their second of eight films together, MacDonald and Eddy traveled to the Canadian wilderness in search of her criminal brother (James Stewart, in his second movie). Along the way they stopped to sing one of their most popular duets, "The Indian Love Call."

MAYTIME (1937): In their hit duet from this picture, Nelson and Jeanette asked each other "Will You Remember?" but there was never any question of their fans forgetting them. This romantic tale of two opera singers and their doomed love was the top-grossing international hit of its year.

SWEETHEARTS (1938): The popular duo didn't always get along offscreen, a situation reflected in the witty script written for this 1938 hit. They were so popular, however, that they were the natural choice to star in MGM's first three-strip Technicolor feature.

Sweethearts

(1938) TITLE LOBBY CARD

THE THIN MAN (1934): This adaptation of Dashiell Hammett's novel made William Powell and Myrna Loy one of MGM's top screen teams, but director W. S. Van Dyke II had to fight to cast them. Mayer thought they were too strongly identified with villainous roles to play the wisecracking husband-and-wife sleuths.

THE GREAT ZIEGFELD (1936): To anchor its most expensive production since *Ben-Hur,* MGM cast William Powell as showman Flo Ziegfeld and Myrna Loy as his second wife, Billie Burke.

AFTER THE THIN MAN (1936): It took two years for MGM to release another Thin Man mystery, but the time was well-spent insuring that the sequel would be as good as the original. In addition to showcasing Powell and Loy, the film provided a juicy, if uncharacteristic role for recent MGM arrival James Stewart.

ANOTHER THIN MAN (1939): After a long illness, Powell returned to the screen in his most popular role, this time adjusting to fatherhood while he and Loy solved a trio of murders.

The Great Ziegfeld
(1936) ONE SHEET

After the Thin Man
(1936) ONE SHEET

Another Thin Man
(1939) ONE SHEET

Libeled Lady

Wife Versus Secretary

MANHATTAN MELODRAMA (1934): Three great stars enlivened this glamorous gangster tale, with Clark Gable as the racketeer prosecuted by former childhood friend Powell, and Loy as the woman torn between the two.

LIBELED LADY (1936): By the mid-thirties, MGM had signed up so many great stars that they could afford to show off a little by putting four of the best into one great movie. Spencer Tracy, Jean Harlow, William Powell, and Myrna Loy joined forces for this spritely newspaper comedy, all about love, lying, and litigation.

WIFE VERSUS SECRETARY (1936): Gable teamed with two of his most popular co-stars, Loy and Jean Harlow, for this spirited romantic comedy. Never the sexpot her publicity made her out to be, Harlow would later say that her role as the simple, virtuous secretary was the closest she ever came to playing herself on screen.

Reckless

(1935) ONE SHEET
ILLUSTRATOR: WILLIAM GALBRAITH CRAWFORD

RED HEADED WOMAN (1932): Harlow's big breakthrough at MGM came when Mayer and Thalberg cast her as the conniving secretary in this sexcharged tale. The film raised censors' hackles around the nation and was banned outright in England.

BOMBSHELL (1933): Harlow spoofed Harlow in this fast-paced comedy about a glamorous star fed up with Hollywood life. In adapting the script from a stage play, writers Jules Furthman and John Lee Mahin played up the parallels to Harlow's career, even showing her at work on a scene from *Red Dust*.

RECKLESS (1935): MGM drew on the tragic life of torch singer Libby Holman for this tale of a Broadway star accused of murder when her husband kills himself. The film had a happy ending off-screen when Harlow fell in love with leading man William Powell.

THE GIRL FROM MISSOURI (1934): With the arrival of stricter Hollywood censorship, MGM was forced to make extensive revisions in this retread of *Red Headed Woman*. Instead of playing a heartless golddigger using sex to get ahead, Harlow became a young beauty determined to keep her virginity until she could land a rich husband.

The Girl from Missouri

(1934) TITLE LOBBY CARD

SUZY (1936): This World War I romance was a mess—cobbled together from scripts by Dorothy Parker and Alan Campbell, Horace Jackson and Lenore Coffee—but the fans loved it. Harlow was a cabaret singer widowed by Irish flyer Franchot Tone, then married to French aviator Cary Grant only to have Tone return from the dead.

RED DUST (1932): MGM had considered this steamy jungle tale for Garbo before casting Clark Gable and Jean Harlow. Harlow completed the film under extreme duress after her husband, MGM executive Paul Bern, died under mysterious circumstances. There were no problems at the box office however, and the studio scored a smash hit.

PERSONAL PROPERTY (1937): Harlow and Robert Taylor made a great love team in this romantic comedy about an American widow in financial difficulties who falls for the man sent to collect on her debts. When she fell ill during the film's publicity tour, however, the stage was set for tragedy.

Suzy

(1936) THREE SHEET

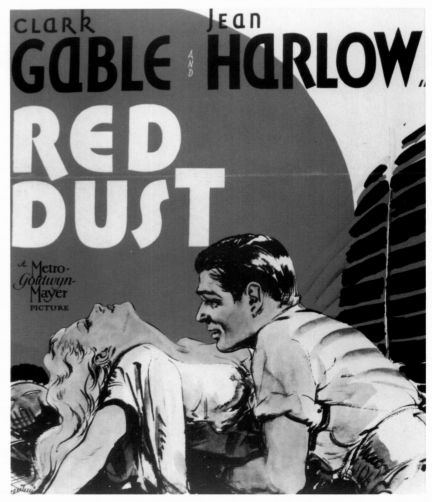

Red Dust

(1932) MINI WINDOW CARD
ILLUSTRATOR: VINCENTINI

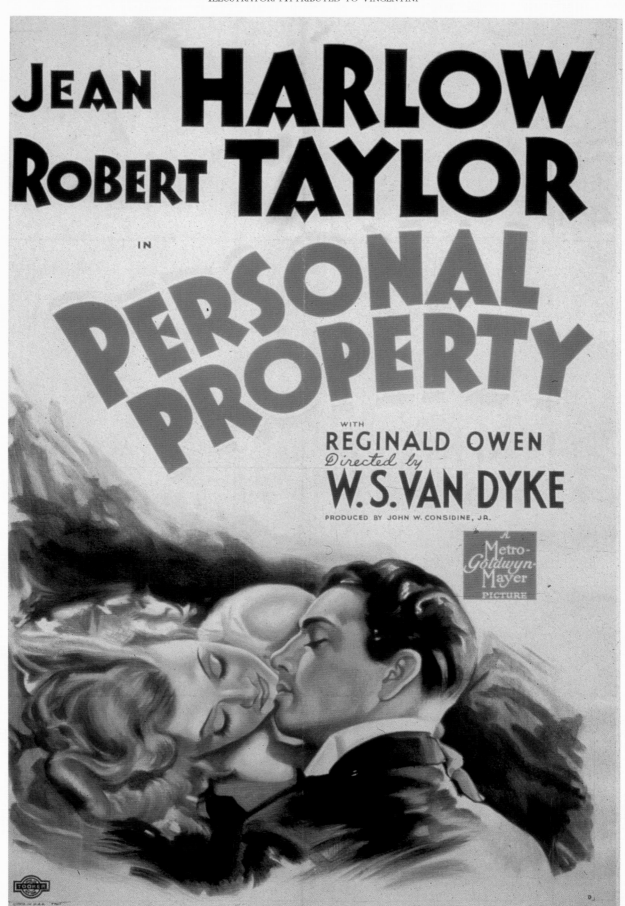

CHINA SEAS (1935): Thalberg had to wait a year to get the stars he wanted for this high-seas adventure, but Gable, Harlow, and Wallace Beery were so perfect for their roles as heroic sea captain, smart-talking blonde, and modern-day pirate that it was worth the wait.

SARATOGA (1937): Although Harlow had not fully recovered from her earlier illness, MGM pushed her into a grueling production schedule on another film co-starring Clark Gable. With a few days left to finish the picture, Harlow grew ill and died at the age of twenty-six.

AFTER OFFICE HOURS (1935): Four years after playing Constance Bennett's brother-in-law in his first MGM film, Gable became her boss and love interest in this crackling newspaper comedy.

HELL DIVERS (1931): In his first year at MGM, Clark Gable made nine films, starting as a supporting player, but his animal magnetism was catching the attention of female fans. Wallace Beery was the nominal star of this nautical drama, but all eyes were on Gable.

Saratoga
(1937) ONE SHEET
ILLUSTRATOR: VINCENTINI

After Office Hours
(1935) THREE SHEET

China Seas
(1935) SIX SHEET

Mutiny on the Bounty
(1935) ONE SHEET
ILLUSTRATOR: ATTRIBUTED TO RALPH ILIGAN

San Francisco
(1936) ONE SHEET
ILLUSTRATOR: RALPH ILIGAN

MUTINY ON THE BOUNTY (1935): MGM may not have dealt directly with the Depression as often as studios like Warner Bros. did, but they found a parallel to contemporary issues in one of the greatest labor-management stories of all time. The result was another big money-maker—and the Oscar for Best Picture.

SAN FRANCISCO (1936): With over $2.2 million in profits, this Barbary Coast epic was Thalberg's most successful film since *The Big Parade*. Jeanette MacDonald was teamed with Gable for the first and only time. Co-star Spencer Tracy won his first Oscar nomination for the film, whose title number would become the city's official anthem.

TOO HOT TO HANDLE (1938): With films like this fast-paced action comedy about rival newsreel reporters, Gable had no trouble bouncing back from the debacle of *Parnell*, one of the few flops of his career. It didn't hurt that this feature was released just after he and co-star Myrna Loy were voted King and Queen of Hollywood in a national poll.

FORSAKING ALL OTHERS (1934): The recently arrived Joseph L. Mankiewicz, who would later write and direct such sophisticated hits as *All About Eve* (1950), gave Crawford, Gable, and Robert Montgomery a glittering script of this comic romance. Gable helps Crawford recover after Montgomery jilts her, only to face losing her when the cad comes back.

LOVE ON THE RUN (1936): Europe may have been ready to burst into flames in the real world, but at MGM it was just a background for fun and games as Gable, Crawford, and Franchot Tone chased each other around the continent. The on-screen romance was matched by the stars' offscreen entanglements, with Crawford playing love scenes opposite current husband Tone and ex-lover Gable.

DANCING LADY (1933): Gable made eight films with Joan Crawford and even had an affair with her. For this backstage musical, she was the star pursued by playboy Franchot Tone, with Gable as the stage manager who really loved her. Somewhere in the chorus, Nelson Eddy made an early screen appearance.

CHAINED (1934): "When she's in his arms, it's the greatest thrill the screen can give!" trumpeted the ads for this shipboard romance in which kept woman Crawford ditches her rich, married boyfriend for hard-working South American rancher Gable.

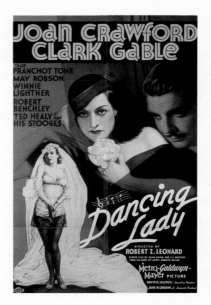

Dancing Lady
(1933) ONE SHEET
ILLUSTRATOR: VINCENTINI

Chained
(1934) ONE SHEET

Love on the Run
(1936) ONE SHEET

OUR BLUSHING BRIDES (1930): For the third of Joan Crawford's flapper films (preceded by *Our Dancing Daughters* in 1928 and *Our Modern Maidens* in 1929), MGM let the star try out a new leading man, Robert Montgomery.

I LIVE MY LIFE (1935): After the success of *Forsaking All Others*, Joseph L. Mankiewicz was assigned to write another Crawford vehicle. Although critics weren't wild about this story, Mayer made Mankiewicz the producer of Crawford's next several films.

THE WOMEN (1939): Critics have called this adaptation of Clare Boothe Luce's stage comedy the funniest film ever made. It's easy to see why, with its all-female cast—including Norma Shearer, Joan Crawford, Rosalind Russell, Paulette Goddard, and Joan Fontaine —working for Hollywood's greatest director of women, George Cukor.

I Live My Life
(1935) ONE SHEET

MANNEQUIN (1937): One of Crawford's specialities was the working-class woman rising to the top through wit, charm, and determination. Rarely did she play the type as well as she did here, teaming with Spencer Tracy for the only time in her career. In the opinion of some observers, watching Tracy at work helped Crawford improve her own acting.

NO MORE LADIES (1935): Crawford was a more level-headed society type in this one, but still foolish enough to think that marriage could reform scoundrel Robert Montgomery. She looked dazzling in her Adrian gowns and got to work with George Cukor, who filled in for a few days when the director, E. H. Griffith, fell ill.

THE ICE FOLLIES OF 1939 (1939): Crawford had studied opera in hopes of moving into Jeanette Mac-Donald's territory, but Mayer vetoed the idea, forcing her into the biggest flop of her career instead. Years later, this would be the film "Crawford" was working on at the start of *Mommie Dearest,* starring Faye Dunaway in an uncanny impersonation of the star.

No More Ladies

(1935) ONE SHEET
ILLUSTRATOR: Vincentini

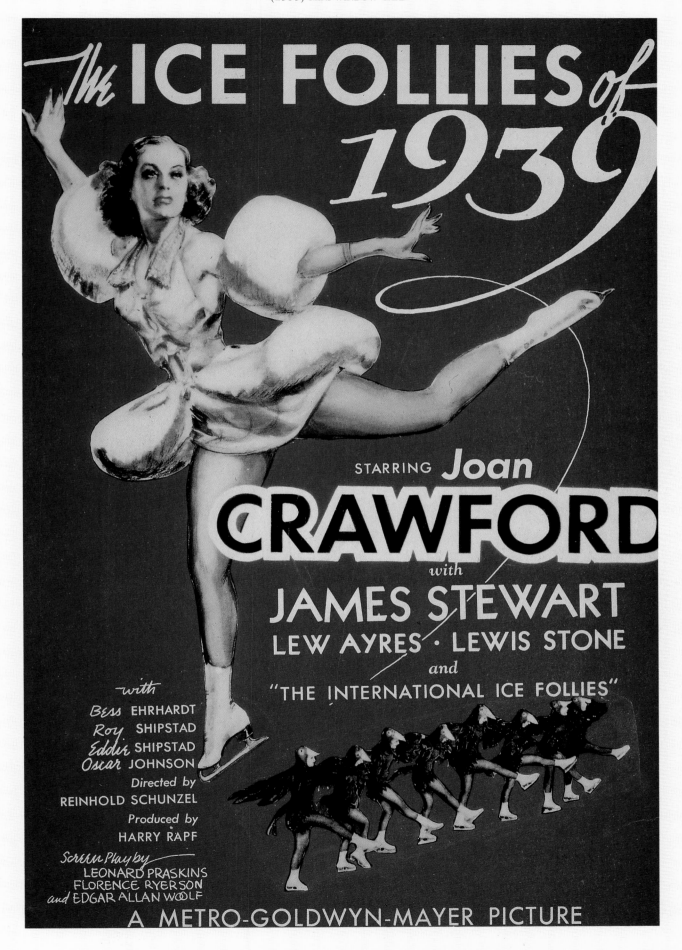

Hide-Out
(1934) ONE SHEET

The Gay Bride
(1934) ONE SHEET

It's a Wonderful World
(1939) ONE SHEET

A YANK AT OXFORD (1937): MGM inaugurated its new British studios with this tale of a brash American oarsman (Robert Taylor) who enrolls at the fabled British university. Prominent in the supporting cast is Vivien Leigh as a flirtatious coed. In fact, some historians claim that David O. Selznick chose her to star in *Gone With the Wind* on the strength of this performance, keeping up the search for Scarlett for publicity purposes only.

HIDE-OUT (1934): Director W. S. Van Dyke II took the one about the farmer's daughter and turned it into popular froth, thanks to a sparkling script and star performances from Robert Montgomery as a racketeer on the lam and Maureen O'Sullivan as the country miss who puts him up and changes his life. Stealing scenes like a seasoned pro was the young Mickey Rooney, still three years away from achieving stardom in the Andy Hardy movies.

THE GAY BRIDE (1934): Carole Lombard, later Mrs. Clark Gable, only made one film for MGM. Her role as a scheming chorus girl who changes her ways when she falls for gangster Chester Morris seemed perfect for Lombard's talents, but the critics were lukewarm.

IT'S A WONDERFUL WORLD (1939): With the screwball comedy cycle dying down, contemporary audiences avoided this charming comedy with Claudette Colbert as a madcap authoress saved from murder charges by James Stewart. In recent years, audiences have rediscovered this minor gem from director W. S. Van Dyke II and writers Ben Hecht and Herman J. Mankiewicz.

A DAY AT THE RACES (1937): The Marx Bros. spent two years testing gags to make sure their second MGM film would be as funny as the first. Again, the studio added a romantic plot and musical numbers, but the highlights were mainly comic, including Chico's turn as a race-track tipster, Groucho's romancing of Margaret Dumont, and Harpo's zany racing finale.

AT THE CIRCUS (1939): Despite some great comic moments—including Groucho's singing of "Lydia, the Tattooed Lady"—the Marx Bros.'s third MGM film had some critics worrying. To many, the studio's strong production values seemed to be intruding on the comedy.

A NIGHT AT THE OPERA (1935): After their last Paramount film, *Duck Soup* (1933), flopped at the box office, many industry insiders thought the Marx Bros. were washed up in pictures. They hadn't reckoned on Irving G. Thalberg, who tamed the trio's anarchic style (at least slightly), threw in some love interest for the humor-impaired, and put them back on top with this wild spoof of the world of grand opera.

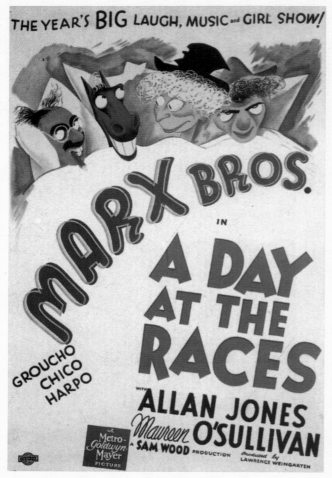

A Day at the Races
(1937) ONE SHEET
ILLUSTRATOR: AL HIRSCHFELD

At the Circus
(1939) THREE SHEET ART
ILLUSTRATOR: AL HIRSCHFELD

The Passionate Plumber

(1932) WINDOW CARD

THE PASSIONATE PLUMBER (1932): With the coming of sound, Buster Keaton lost control of his films to Thalberg, Mayer, and a string of producers who didn't seem to understand his genius. This adaptation of *Her Cardboard Lover* did well at the box-office, but was a far cry from previous triumphs in quality or the opportunities it gave the star for his particular brand of slapstick comedy.

WHAT! NO BEER? (1933): Within two years, studio meddling and his own alcoholism destroyed Keaton's career. In his last MGM film, he wound up playing second banana to second-billed Jimmy Durante. Keaton would return to MGM in the forties to play small roles, write gags, and help develop the comedic talents of such stars as Red Skelton and Lucille Ball.

THE DEVIL'S BROTHER (1933): The great comedy team of Laurel and Hardy made many short films for MGM, but also starred in a few features like *The Devil's Brother*. Produced by Hal Roach, this adaptation of an Auber operetta was one of their best.

What! No Beer?

(1933) TITLE LOBBY CARD
ILLUSTRATOR: AL HIRSCHFELD

TREASURE ISLAND (1934): Although they made three films together, Wallace Beery and Jackie Cooper were hardly friends. The child actor was afraid of his co-star, while Beery resented the youth's natural scene-stealing ability.

CAPTAINS COURAGEOUS (1937): Spencer Tracy hated his performance as Manuel, the Portuguese fisherman, in this adaptation of Rudyard Kipling's novel, particularly after Joan Crawford took one look at him in his curly wig and shouted, "Hello, Harpo!" But the film won him his first Oscar for Best Actor and was a big winner at the box office. Lionel Barrymore, Mickey Rooney, and Freddie Bartholomew co-starred.

DAVID COPPERFIELD (1935): Producer David O. Selznick set a new standard for Hollywood adaptations of the classics with this faithful rendition of Dickens's sprawling novel. Helping tremendously was George Cukor's direction and the strong cast.

David Copperfield
(1935) ONE SHEET
ILLUSTRATOR: ARMANDO SEGUSO

Captains Courageous
(1937) MINI WINDOW CARD
ILLUSTRATOR: VINCENTINI

GREATER THAN "DAVID COPPERFIELD"

Charles Dickens'

A CHRISTMAS CAROL

with

REGINALD OWEN
GENE LOCKHART
KATHLEEN LOCKHART
TERRY KILBURN
BARRY MACKAY
LYNNE CARVER

SCREEN PLAY BY HUGO BUTLER · PRODUCED BY JOSEPH L. MANKIEWICZ
DIRECTED BY EDWIN L. MARIN

A Metro-Goldwyn-Mayer PICTURE

The Good Earth

(1937) THREE SHEET

Goodbye Mr. Chips

(1939) MINI WINDOW CARD

A CHRISTMAS CAROL (1938): This holiday classic was inspired by Lionel Barrymore's annual readings of the Dickens classic on the radio, but by the time filming began, the actor was too crippled with arthritis to play the role. His friend Reginald Owen took over, delivering his best performance as cranky old Ebenezer Scrooge.

THE GOOD EARTH (1937): Pearl Buck's novel made for sumptuous filmmaking, with Paul Muni starring and Luise Rainer winning an Oscar for her almost silent performance. The film was made on such a grand scale, however, that it failed to recoup its cost until years later.

A TALE OF TWO CITIES (1935): Selznick soon tired of jokes about his relationship to Louis B. Mayer ("The son-in-law also rises," quipped some) and left to form his own independent production company. For his final MGM production, he returned to Dickens, assembling a dream cast that included Ronald Colman, Lewis Stone, and Isabel Jewell.

GOODBYE MR. CHIPS (1939): Robert Donat may have won an Oscar for his performance as the gentle schoolteacher, but Greer Garson, as his wife, would become queen of the lot, replacing the soon-to-retire Greta Garbo and Norma Shearer. She had been hand-picked for the role—and for stardom—by Mayer, who was enchanted with her ladylike demeanor.

A Tale of Two Cities

(1935) ONE SHEET
ILLUSTRATOR: VINCENTINI

85

The Wizard of Oz
(1939) INSERT

THE WIZARD OF OZ (1939): This musical fantasy was originally planned as MGM's prestige production for the year; a film that would bring credit, but no great profit to the studio. Instead, it became a milestone: the picture that made Judy Garland a major star and introduced her signature tune, "Over the Rainbow"; and the film that introduced MGM's most important producer of the forties, Arthur Freed (although the fledgling had to start as an assistant to established producer-director Mervyn LeRoy). A comparative financial failure on its initial release, *The Wizard of Oz* has become a timeless favorite and traditional holiday classic.

The Wizard of Oz

(1939) SIX SHEET
ILLUSTRATOR: AL HIRSCHFELD

Gone With the Wind
(1939) ONE SHEET

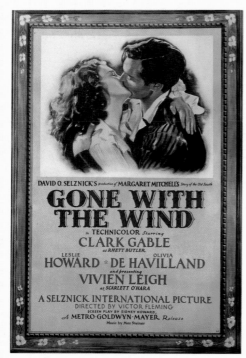

Gone With the Wind

(1939) ONE SHEET

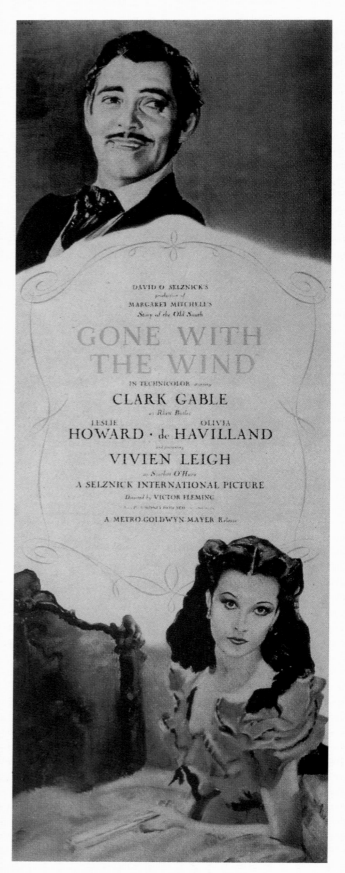

Gone With the Wind

(1939) INSERT

GONE WITH THE WIND (1939): David O. Selznick turned Margaret Mitchell's sprawling novel into the greatest achievement in Hollywood's history, complete with immortal performances, breathtaking action, and heart-stopping romance. The film was MGM's only tangentially; Selznick traded distribution rights to MGM in return for partial backing and Clark Gable's services. It could have been MGM's in toto, but Irving G. Thalberg turned the story down before it got to Selznick, claiming that "No Civil War picture ever made a dime."

The Forties

ALTHOUGH THE WAR IN EUROPE was initially costly for MGM and the rest of Hollywood—eleven nations were closed to American film product—it soon led to unprecedented box-office figures on the homefront. Wartime audiences turned to the movies for re-creations of overseas action or for relief from the horrors in the headlines. ❊ MGM met the demand with a string of escapist hits and a horde of new stars. Mayer's personal discovery, Greer Garson, personified English gentility under fire. Van Johnson was the all-American boy, and June Allyson was the girl every GI had left behind. Mickey Rooney and Judy Garland cracked the box-office top ten by personifying youthful, all-American exuberance. Esther Williams gave wholesomeness a new name as the star of a series of aquatic festivals. ❊ At the same time, MGM lost some of its biggest stars of earlier years. Greta Garbo and Norma Shearer retired while still at the top. Joan Crawford left MGM for Warner Bros. Top male stars like Clark Gable, Robert Taylor, and James Stewart went off to battle, while Myrna Loy left MGM for the Red Cross. ❊ World War II changed the world, though it took MGM a long time to notice. When Gable, Loy, and Taylor returned to the studio (Stewart's contract had run out), MGM pushed them into the same types of romances and comedies they had made in the thirties, but this time the audience wasn't buying. ❊ The one exception to this downward trend was the MGM musical, particularly as produced by Arthur Freed. Building a production unit that included director Vincente Minnelli, dancer Gene Kelly, choreographer Stanley Donen, and numerous other impressive talents, he produced a series of sophisticated, elegant musicals that were the envy of the world. ❊ With the end of wartime prosperity, MGM began to falter. Since Thalberg's death, Mayer had run the studio through a committee of producers, an increasingly cumbersome structure that resulted in rising costs that cut into the studio's diminishing profits still further. Finally, Loew's, Inc. President Nicholas Schenck ordered Mayer to find a new Thalberg. ❊ The lucky (or unlucky) heir to the throne was Dore Schary, an Oscar-winning writer (for MGM's *Boy's Town*) who had moved into production, first with David O. Selznick and then as head of RKO. When he quarreled with that studio's new owner, Howard Hughes, he was ready for a move to MGM. ❊ At first everything was fine between Mayer and his new production chief, but conflict was inevitable. Liberal-minded Schary liked to insert social messages into his films; conservative Mayer insisted on sticking to escapism. The stage was set for a confrontation that would change the face of MGM forever.

STRIKE UP THE BAND (1940): Mickey and Judy had another hit as teens putting together a big dance band. The film marked Judy's first encounter with future husband Vincente Minnelli, who helped stage an imaginative sequence in which Rooney turns a bowl of fruit into an animated band.

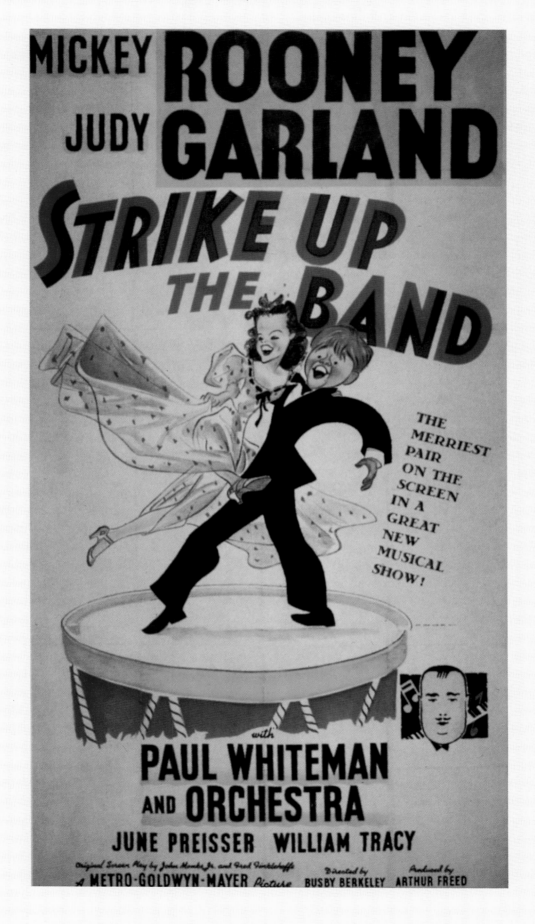

The Mortal Storm

(1940) ONE SHEET
ILLUSTRATOR: ARMANDO SEGUSO

Journey for Margaret

(1943) ONE SHEET
ILLUSTRATOR: VINCENTINI

THE MOST EXCITING PICTURE!

THE MORTAL STORM

Starring

MARGARET SULLAVAN
JAMES STEWART
ROBERT YOUNG
FRANK MORGAN

with ROBERT STACK · BONITA GRANVILLE
IRENE RICH · WILLIAM T. ORR
MARIA OUSPENSKAYA · GENE REYNOLDS

A Frank BORZAGE Production
A METRO-GOLDWYN-MAYER Picture

THE MORTAL STORM (1940): Joseph Goebbels banned all MGM pictures from German-occupied territories after the studio released this tale of a family torn apart by Nazi persecution in the thirties. Ironically, the script never identified Germany as the location for all this heartache. James Stewart and Margaret Sullavan starred.

JOURNEY FOR MARGARET (1943): U.S. involvement in World War II plunged Hollywood into the war effort as MGM and other studios churned out films in support of the Allies. This touching story of a British war orphan made a star out of Margaret O'Brien.

THE SEVENTH CROSS (1944): Spencer Tracy's largely silent peformance was the glue holding together this suspense picture about a conentration camp escapee's journey to freedom. Among the colorful character's helping and hindering him were offscreen husband and wife Hume Cronyn and Jessica Tandy, the latter in her film debut.

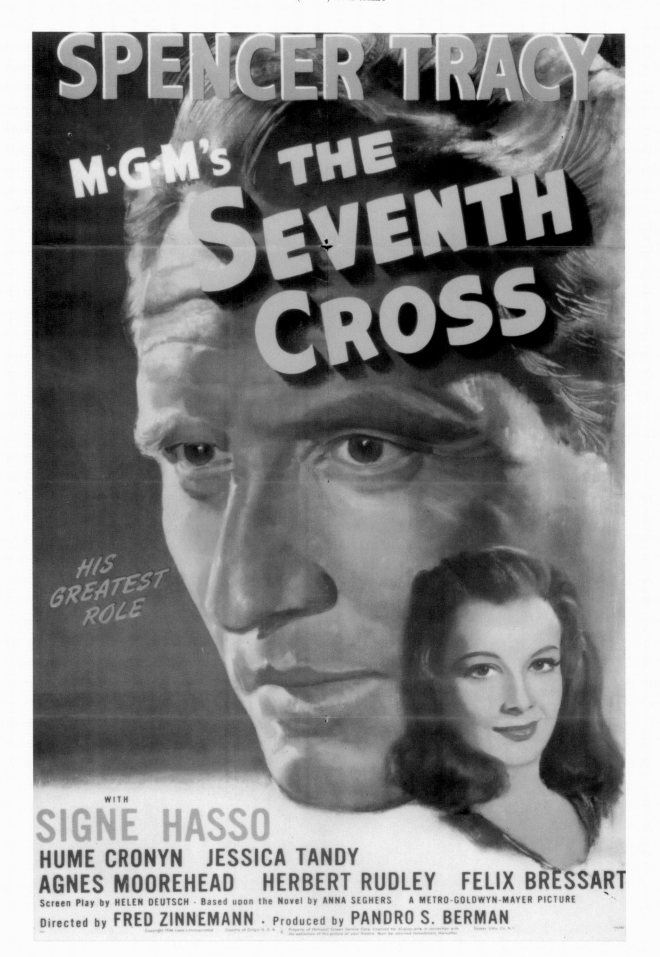

THE CLOCK (1945): Judy Garland made her only non-musical film at MGM with this story of a young woman who marries a soldier (Robert Walker) during a whirlwind forty-eight-hour leave. Director Vincente Minnelli captured the film's New York background perfectly without ever leaving MGM's Culver City backlot.

COMMAND DECISION (1948): The post-war years brought a more somber look at U.S. military maneuvers. Clark Gable gave one of his best performances as a flight commander forced to send his men on a series of suicide missions over Germany.

ESCAPE (1940): The war in Europe finally made its way to Culver City in 1940, with Norma Shearer as a German countess helping American Robert Taylor rescue his mother (Alla Nazimova) from a concentration camp. Making his American film debut was a German actor noted for his opposition to the Nazis, the great Conrad Veidt.

WATERLOO BRIDGE (1940): Although this hit love story was set in World War I, it was a forerunner of the wartime romances that would become a Hollywood staple during World War II. In her follow-up to *Gone With the Wind*, Vivien Leigh proved she was no flash in the pan, though she was disappointed that Robert Taylor, rather than her husband, Laurence Olivier, was the leading man here.

Two-Faced Woman

(1941) ONE SHEET
ILLUSTRATOR: SOTERO FOR CARICATURE

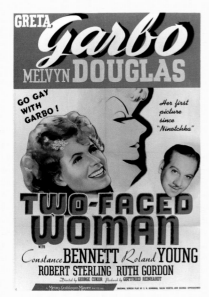

TWO-FACED WOMAN (1941): This box-office flop about a woman pretending to be her glamorous twin sister so she could seduce her own husband was Garbo's screen swan song at the age of thirty six. Originally, she had only planned to take a vacation until the European market reopened at the end of World War II. But the longer she stayed away, the harder it was to come back.

WE WERE DANCING (1941): Norma Shearer didn't want to play a woman with a grown son, so she turned down *Mrs. Miniver* for this frothy box-office flop. With the failure of her next film, *Her Cardboard Lover* (1942), Shearer retired from the screen while still a star.

We Were Dancing

(1941) ONE SHEET

Gaslight
(1944) SIX SHEET

GASLIGHT (1944): Ingrid Bergman paid a visit to MGM when Hedy Lamarr turned down the chance to be driven mad by Charles Boyer in this Victorian melodrama. She even collected an Oscar for her troubles. Director George Cukor made this one of the best films of its year, with Oscar nominations going to Boyer and, in an amazing film debut, Angela Lansbury.

Clark Joan
GABLE · CRAWFORD
IN
STRANGE CARGO

with **IAN HUNTER** PETER **LORRE**

PAUL **LUKAS** Albert **DEKKER** J. Edward **BROMBERG**

Eduardo **CIANNELLI** A *Frank* **BORZAGE** Production

SCREEN PLAY BY LAWRENCE HAZARD · BASED ON THE BOOK
"NOT TOO NARROW, NOT TOO DEEP" BY RICHARD SALE
Directed by FRANK BORZAGE
PRODUCED BY JOSEPH L. MANKIEWICZ

A *Metro-Goldwyn-Mayer* PICTURE

STRANGE CARGO (1940): Although Joan Crawford had been named box-office poison in a late thirties exhibitors ad, MGM kept renewing her contract. The studio seemed bent on proving the exhibitors right with films like this turgid prison-escape tale co-starring Clark Gable. The film's treatment of religion was so outré that the Legion of Decency threatened it with a condemned rating.

A WOMAN'S FACE (1941): Ironically, as Crawford's star was falling, MGM gave her one of her best films, a remake of a Swedish thriller that had originally starred Ingrid Bergman as a scarred woman who loses her criminal tendencies when a plastic surgeon turns her into a beauty. Under George Cukor's direction, Crawford delivered her best performance at the studio.

REUNION IN FRANCE (1943): If, as some suspected, Louis B. Mayer was sending Crawford bad scripts to get her to walk out on her contract, he couldn't have done better than he did with this one. She starred as a Parisian fashion designer who joins the Resistance after rescuing downed American flyer John Wayne. After one more embarrassment, *Beyond Suspicion* (1943), Crawford left MGM.

WHEN LADIES MEET (1942): With the retirement of Garbo and Norma Shearer, Crawford had hoped to become the new queen of the lot. Instead, Mayer gave Greer Garson first pick of choice properties. The two locked horns on screen only once, in this adaptation of Rachel Crothers' hit comedy.

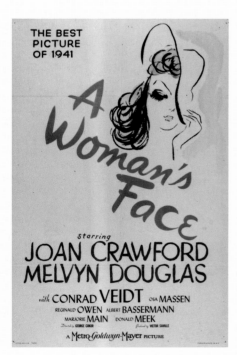

A Woman's Face

(1941) ONE SHEET

Reunion in France

(1943) THREE SHEET

When Ladies Meet

(1942) ONE SHEET

MAISIE WAS A LADY (1940): Ann Sothern went domestic for one of the best in the "Maisie" series. Taking a job as a house maid, she solves the problems of her rich employers and their friends, including Lew Ayres and Maureen O'Sullivan.

TARZAN'S SECRET TREASURE (1941): With increasing focus on Boy and Cheetah, the *Tarzan* series had become kiddie fare by the forties. This fast-paced account of the discovery of gold in the jungle king's backyard pulled in the fans, but Maureen O'Sullivan was tiring of the series and wanted out.

TARZAN'S NEW YORK ADVENTURE (1942): The studio got Maureen O'Sullivan to make one more *Tarzan* film by sending the jungle family to Manhattan, where she got to model some chic contemporary fashions. But the move also reflected MGM's inability to create fresh plots for the jungle lord. Instead, they sold Johnny Weissmuller and Johnny Sheffield's contracts to RKO, where the series would continue without O'Sullivan.

Tarzan's New York Adventure

(1942) SIX SHEET

SON OF LASSIE (1945): MGM's most prolific animal star of the forties was Lad, a male collie masquerading as the heroic female. The pup went off to war in this entry, meeting Peter Lawford and future television co-star June Lockhart along the way.

NATIONAL VELVET (1944): At RKO, producer Pandro S. Berman was looking for a Katharine Hepburn vehicle when he first bought the rights to Enid Bagnold's novel about a young girl and her horse. By the time MGM brought the book to the screen, Elizabeth Taylor was the perfect age to play Velvet Brown. Mickey Rooney, Anne Revere, and Angela Lansbury co-starred.

THE YEARLING (1946): It took two tries to bring to the screen Marjorie Kinnan Rawlings' story of a boy and his pet deer. The first company, with Spencer Tracy and Anne Revere as the boy's parents, fell victim to bad weather on the Florida Everglades location and a bad relationship between Tracy and director Victor Fleming. Five years later, Clarence Brown took Gregory Peck and Jane Wyman through the story to stunning effect.

NORTHWEST PASSAGE (1940): Before the U.S. entry into World War II, historical epics like this gave audiences a sense of what they would soon be fighting for. It had taken MGM two years to bring Kenneth Roberts' best-seller to the screen. The book was so sprawling that the studio decided to halt production midway through the action, adding a subtitle, "Book 1—Rogers' Rangers," promising a sequel that would never be made.

3 GODFATHERS (1948): Westerns were hardly MGM's forte, but when the studio pulled out the stops on one, they usually came up with a winner. This was the sixth screen version of Frank B. Kyne's story about three outlaws who deliver a baby in the desert and risk their lives taking it to safety in New Jerusalem. With John Ford directing John Wayne, it was also the best.

THE BAD MAN (1941): This was another tried and true tale, filmed twice previously. In addition, it allowed Wallace Beery to play a softer version of the good-bad bandito he had scored with in 1934's *Viva Villa!* Future president Ronald Reagan paid a rare visit to MGM, on loan from Warner Bros., to co-star as the young cowhand Beery takes under his wing.

Northwest Passage

(1940) ONE SHEET

3 Godfathers

(1948) TITLE LOBBY CARD

THE BIG STORE (1941): The Marx Brothers ran rampant in a department store for their last MGM feature. Although Groucho had Margaret Dumont to romance, and the team had a rousing production number in "Sing While You Sell," they were tired of what they felt were increasingly pedestrian studio features. This was their last MGM film and their last feature for five years.

BUD ABBOTT AND LOU COSTELLO IN HOLLYWOOD (1945): Former burlesque clowns Bud Abbott and Lou Costello were the top-grossing comedy team of the forties and the only stars ever to get their complete names in a film's title. In the last of their three MGM pictures, they played small-time agents, providing the perfect excuse for a tour of the studio backlot, with cameo appearances by Lucille Ball, Butch Jenkins and director Robert Z. Leonard.

The Big Store
(1941) ONE SHEET

BITTER SWEET (1940): The Eddy-MacDonald team met critical resistance with this adaptation of Noël Coward's stage classic when some writers noted that the leads were clearly too old for their roles as young innocents. Box-office receipts were down and dipped even more with the stars' next film, *I Married an Angel* (1942), bringing an end to the once-profitable pairing.

NEW MOON (1940): Nelson Eddy and Jeanette MacDonald started the decade with Sigmund Romberg's rousing operetta about 18th-century rebels in the Louisiana bayou. The score included such favorites as "Stout Hearted Men," "Wanting You," and "Lover Come Back."

SMILIN' THROUGH (1941): Jeanette MacDonald traded on-screen-love Nelson Eddy for off-screen-husband Gene Raymond in an effort to break out on her own with a musical version of this perennial tear-jerker. Norma Talmadge had filmed a silent version in 1922, while Norma Shearer had had one of her biggest hits with the story in 1932.

New Moon

(1940) TITLE LOBBY CARD

KATHLEEN (1941): As a child, Shirley Temple had been the top box-office star of the thirties at 20th Century-Fox, but she was a has-been by age 12. MGM signed her to a one-year contract with great fanfare, then couldn't find the right picture for her. They finally dumped her into this minor domestic comedy, dubbed her one vocal number and let her contract lapse.

LADY BE GOOD (1941): Producer Arthur Freed had so much talent at his disposal that all he needed for a hit was a few hand-chosen stars, a couple of great songs, and the barest bones of a story—in this case the adventures of married songwriters Ann Sothern and Robert Young as they put on a show. Highlights include Eleanor Powell's tap solo to "Fascinating Rhythm" and the Oscar-winning "The Last Time I Saw Paris."

THE CHOCOLATE SOLDIER (1941): For his part, Nelson Eddy tried a series of new singing partners, including Metropolitan Opera star Risë Stevens. Despite the title, the film used only a few songs from Oscar Straus' popular operetta. The plot was taken from another MGM film, *The Guardsman* (1931), with jealous husband Eddy masquerading as a Russian soldier to test Stevens' fidelity.

The Chocolate Soldier
(1941) INSERT

Lady Be Good
(1941) ONE SHEET

111

DU BARRY WAS A LADY (1943): Cole Porter's stage hit provided Freed with another winner, with Red Skelton as a nightclub waiter who dreams he's Louis XIV, singing star Lucille Ball as his mistress, and hoofer Gene Kelly as a dashing rebel. This was one of the first MGM films for future director Charles Walters, who had played Kelly's role on Broadway and served as dance director here.

BEST FOOT FORWARD (1943): June Allyson made her screen debut as a singing coed whose life is thrown in turmoil when a movie star (Lucille Ball, playing herself) shows up to attend a military school dance. Harry James played his version of "Flight of the Bumblebee," while Allyson and the other students strutted their stuff on the popular "Buckle Down, Winsocki."

ZIEGFELD FOLLIES (1946): Freed spent two years in production on this all-star review, the first plotless MGM musical since 1929's *Hollywood Revue*. Among the stars in a series of lavish numbers and sketches were Gene Kelly, Lena Horne, Lucille Ball, Esther Williams, and best of all, Judy Garland in a musical send-up of Greer Garson that originally had been written for the British star herself.

CABIN IN THE SKY (1943): Vincente Minnelli made his film directing debut with this stylish rendition of the hit Broadway musical, MGM's first all-black feature since *Hallelujah* (1929). Lena Horne, Ethel Waters, Louis Armstrong, and Eddie "Rochester" Anderson socked across songs like "Taking a Chance on Love" and "Happiness Is a Thing Called Joe."

Du Barry Was a Lady
(1943) ONE SHEET
ILLUSTRATOR: MARCEL VERTÈS

Ziegfeld Follies
(1946) ONE SHEET
ILLUSTRATOR: GEORGE PETTY

Best Foot Forward
(1943) ONE SHEET

Till the Clouds Roll By

(1946) ONE SHEET

ILLUSTRATOR: AL HIRSCHFELD

A Date with Judy

(1948) ONE SHEET

THOUSANDS CHEER (1943): MGM joined the other studios producing star-studded wartime musicals with this tale of a headstrong trapeze artist (Gene Kelly) who gets involved in an all-star show for the men on their way overseas. With Mickey Rooney, Judy Garland, Lena Horne and Red Skelton among the guest stars, the film was a big box-office winner.

TILL THE CLOUDS ROLL BY (1946): Biographies of Broadway composers like Jerome Kern gave MGM and Arthur Freed the chance to spotlight a variety of musical stars. Judy Garland took top honors for her cameo as Marilyn Miller, with scenes directed by an uncredited Vincente Minnelli. Garland would later laugh that she was visibly pregnant (with Liza) when she sang "Who Stole my Heart Away?"

WORDS AND MUSIC (1948): Freed's all-star tribute to songwriters Richard Rodgers and Lorenz Hart (Tom Drake and Mickey Rooney) had a stronger script than *Till the Clouds Roll By* and even better musical numbers, including Judy Garland singing "Johnny One Note," Lena Horne belting out "The Lady is a Tramp," June Allyson and the Blackburn Twins scoring a big hit on "Thou Swell," and Gene Kelly and Vera-Ellen dazzling audiences in an eight-minute ballet set to "Slaughter on Tenth Avenue."

A DATE WITH JUDY (1948): Elizabeth Taylor and Jane Powell rose to star status with the success of this charming teen musical in which the two vie for playboy Robert Stack, and Powell suspects father Wallace Beery of having an affair with Carmen Miranda. In the first of two films with MGM, the Brazilian bombshell introduced one of her biggest hits, "Cuanto Me Gusta."

ANCHORS AWEIGH (1945): Gene Kelly's big breakthrough as a star came with this imaginative tale of two sailors (Kelly and top-billed Frank Sinatra) helping a film extra (Kathryn Grayson) get her own big break. Kelly's dance numbers, particularly a duet with Jerry the Mouse from the studio's popular cartoon series, helped make the film a hit and won him a surprise Oscar nomination for Best Actor.

THE KISSING BANDIT (1947): MGM bought Frank Sinatra's contract from RKO in 1944, hoping to make the bobby-soxers' delight a solid addition to their stable of musical talent. However, aside from putting him in three films with Gene Kelly, the studio never seemed to know what to do with him. This ridiculous film was the nadir of his MGM days, enlivened only by a dance number featuring guest stars Cyd Charisse, Ann Miller, and Ricardo Montalban.

ON THE TOWN (1949): As the decade ended, Freed, Gene Kelly, and director-choreographer Stanley Donen ushered in a new era for the Hollywood musical. Not only did Kelly and co-stars Frank Sinatra, Ann Miller, Vera-Ellen, Betty Garrett, and Jules Munshin travel to New York to shoot some numbers on location, but co-directors Kelly and Donen made every effort to create a seamless blend in which script and songs flowed effortlessly into one another.

The Kissing Bandit
(1947) ONE SHEET

LITTLE NELLIE KELLY (1940): Judy Garland took a stab at adult acting, albeit briefly, in this adaptation of the George M. Cohan stage hit. In a double role she played an Irish immigrant who dies in childbirth and the woman's daughter.

ZIEGFELD GIRL (1941): MGM gave Garland the glamor treatment, casting her with Lana Turner and Hedy Lamarr in this lavish musical about the career and romantic trials of three chorus girls. Although she was clearly the juvenile in the group, playing puppy-love scenes with young Jackie Cooper, the nineteen-year-old star shocked fans and family by running off to marry composer David Rose shortly after this film was completed.

BABES ON BROADWAY (1941): It took a while for Garland's screen roles to catch up with her offscreen maturity, but that wasn't a problem when the films were as good as this one. The best of the Mickey and Judy "puttin'-on-a-show" musicals gave the team a hit with "How About You?" and included a number in which Rooney spoofed Carmen Miranda.

Babes on Broadway

(1941) TITLE LOBBY CARD

FOR ME AND MY GAL (1942): Garland finally moved into adult roles as a vaudevillian in love with unscrupulous hoofer Gene Kelly, in his film debut. Critics were impressed with the acting of both stars. Kelly would always credit his co-star with helping him adjust to film acting.

PRESENTING LILY MARS (1943): That Garland could carry a picture on her own was amply demonstrated by this high-grossing, uneven tale of a small-town girl who dreams of Broadway stardom. The highlight was Garland's duet with Connie Gilchrist, as a onetime-star-turned-cleaning-woman.

GIRL CRAZY (1943): Garland and Rooney starred together in this Wild West musical with songs by George and Ira Gershwin, including "Embraceable You," "But Not for Me," and an eye-popping Busby Berkeley staging of "I Got Rhythm." This was Garland's last film with the legendary director-choreographer who had staged some of her best early musicals.

Presenting Lily Mars

(1943) HALF-SHEET

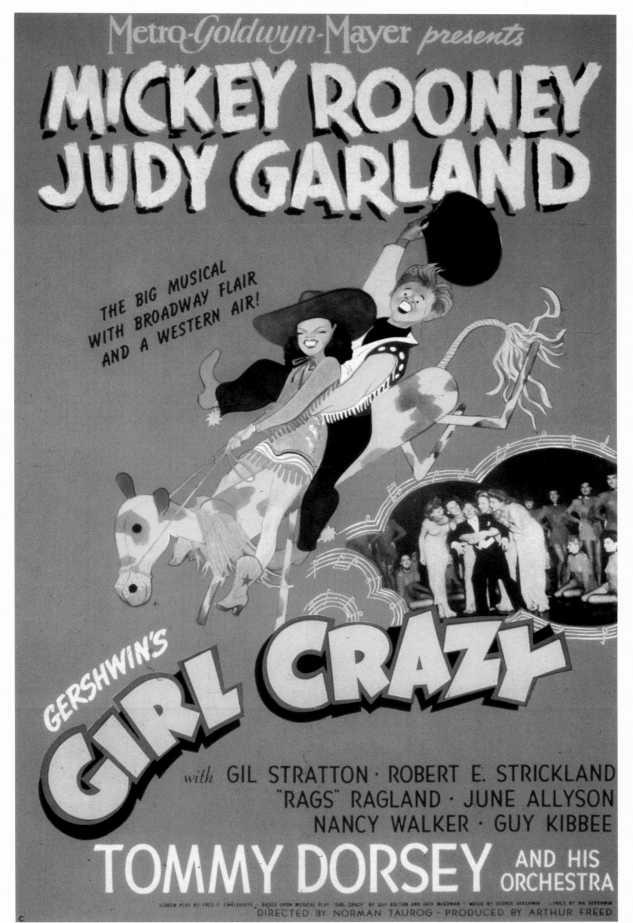

MEET ME IN ST. LOUIS (1944): Garland gave her best performance to date—some would call it her best ever—in this charming period musical, helped immeasurably by the guidance of producer Arthur Freed and director Vincente Minnelli. Initially, the star didn't care for her new director, but as they worked together on the role, the two fell in love.

THE HARVEY GIRLS (1946): Garland was so popular that people hissed Angela Lansbury in public for being mean to the star on-screen. This musical western gave Garland some memorable comic bits and another big hit with the Oscar-winning "On the Atchison, Topeka and Santa Fe."

THE PIRATE (1948): With Garland back above the title (after taking time off to give birth to daughter Liza), and the star reteamed with Gene Kelly and Vincente Minnelli, this Caribbean-set musical should have been a bigger hit, but it was too sophisticated to do well in the sticks. It also marked the start of the emotional problems that would seriously damage Garland's film career. Her marriage was faltering, and she would request that Minnelli be replaced as director of her next film, *Easter Parade* (1948).

The Harvey Girls

(1946) ONE SHEET

ANDY HARDY MEETS DEBUTANTE (1940): Judy Garland returned to the Hardy series for this tale of Andy's misconceived crush on a high-society woman. In the latter role, Diana Lewis made a strong impression shortly before retiring from the screen to become Mrs. William Powell, a role she would play for the rest of her life.

LIFE BEGINS FOR ANDY HARDY (1941): "Andy Hardy Grows Up" would have described this entry in the series better. Along with getting a lecture about the birds and the bees from Judge Hardy (Lewis Stone), Andy had to deal with life in the big city and the advances of a love-hungry divorcée. Fortunately, the Judge and Betsy Booth (Judy Garland, in her last Hardy movie) came to the rescue.

ANDY HARDY'S DOUBLE LIFE (1943): The Hardy series' usefulness as a testing ground for new contract players was amply demonstrated when Mickey Rooney went swimming with the young Esther Williams a year before she side-stroked her way to stardom in *Bathing Beauty*.

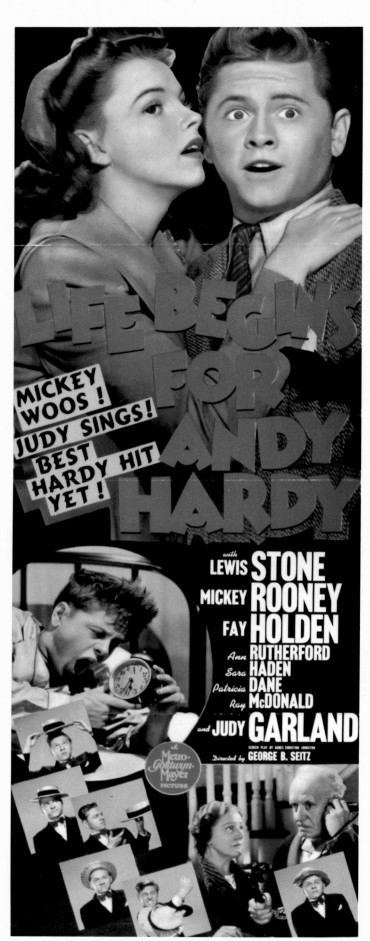

Andy Hardy Meets Debutante
(1940) ONE SHEET

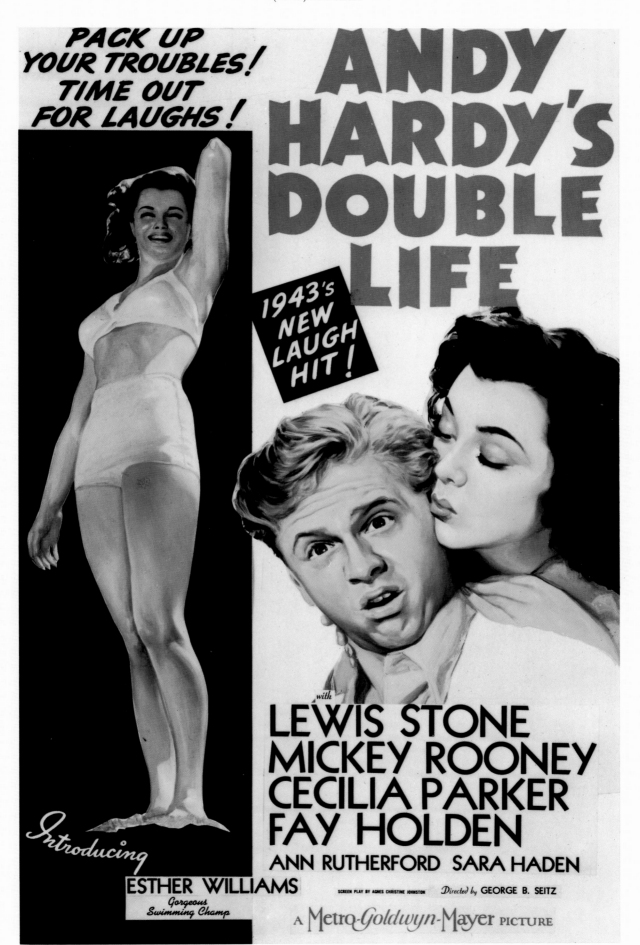

PACK UP YOUR TROUBLES! TIME OUT FOR LAUGHS!

ANDY HARDY'S DOUBLE LIFE

1943's NEW LAUGH HIT!

Introducing ESTHER WILLIAMS *Gorgeous Swimming Champ*

with
LEWIS STONE
MICKEY ROONEY
CECILIA PARKER
FAY HOLDEN
ANN RUTHERFORD SARA HADEN

SCREEN PLAY BY AGNES CHRISTINE JOHNSTON *Directed by* GEORGE B. SEITZ

A Metro-Goldwyn-Mayer PICTURE

BATHING BEAUTY (1944): When MGM promoted Esther Williams to star status for this film, they didn't take any chances. Along with two swimming numbers for the star, they threw in Red Skelton for box-office insurance and imported a bevy of guest musical performers, including band-leaders Harry James and Xavier Cugat, vocalist Helen Forrest, and organist Ethel Smith.

THIS TIME FOR KEEPS (1947): In most of her films, Williams starred in a simple romantic story that left room for her water ballets and left the singing, dancing and comedy for other players. The critics thought it was silly, but the fans ate it up. Here, she co-starred with Jimmy Durante, Xavier Cugat and Metropolitan Opera tenor Lauritz Melchior, who had a brief fling as an MGM star.

ON AN ISLAND WITH YOU (1947): Williams' swimming numbers usually provided a good excuse for exotic locales, like the Hawaiian setting for this musical. Durante and Cugat were back for laughs and Latin rhythms, with Peter Lawford as the love interest.

The Shop Around the Corner
(1940) ONE SHEET
ILLUSTRATORS: ARMANDO SEGUSO FOR PORTRAIT AND
WILLIAM GALBRAITH CRAWFORD FOR CARTOON

I Love You Again
(1940) ONE SHEET

THE SHOP AROUND THE CORNER (1940): A sterling example of director Ernst Lubitsch's way with wit and charm, this delightful tale of coworkers in a small Budapest shop who do not realize they are pen pals helped make big stars out of James Stewart and Margaret Sullavan.

I LOVE YOU AGAIN (1940): MGM's other top screen team, William Powell and Myrna Loy, continued undiminished into the forties. The reason was top scripts like this one, in which Powell recovers from eight years of amnesia and reveals his true, madcap personality to wife Loy.

SHADOW OF THE THIN MAN (1941): Not all the stars going off to war in the forties were men. After finishing the fourth entry in the Thin Man series, Loy left MGM and the screen for three years to work with the American Red Cross. The studio briefly considered recasting the role with contract star Marsha Hunt, then realized that Loy was irreplaceable and waited for her to return.

PRIDE AND PREJUDICE (1940): Greer Garson's star continued to rise when MGM paired her with Laurence Olivier in this elegant adaptation of Jane Austen's classic. The studio sold the early 19th-century comedy of manners in strictly contemporary terms, with ads blazoning: "Five charming sisters on the gayest, merriest manhunt that ever snared a bewildered bachelor! Girls! Take a lesson from these husband hunters."

BLOSSOMS IN THE DUST (1941): Garson got a major boost out of this sentimental biography of Edna Gladney, the Texas woman who fought a long battle to protect the rights of adopted children. Not only did the film team her for the first time with frequent co-star Walter Pidgeon, but its heart-tugging plot made her a major box-office star.

MRS. MINIVER (1942): President Franklin Roosevelt and Winston Churchill credited MGM with swaying public opinion in support of England's war effort with this tale of a middle-class British family coping with the realities of World War II. The film also marked the zenith of the Garson-Pidgeon team, with Garson winning one of the film's seven Oscars.

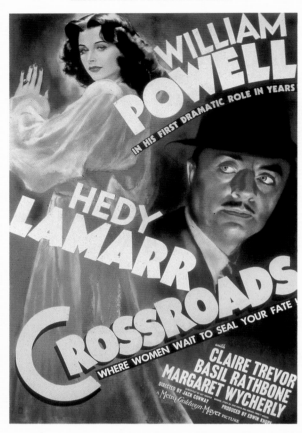

CROSSROADS (1942): Like many a star, Lamarr contributed to the war effort by starring in anti-Nazi films like this thriller in which William Powell played her husband, an American diplomat fighting German spies in Paris. The beautiful star was even more helpful when she sold kisses to sell war bonds—at $25,000 a pop.

THE HEAVENLY BODY (1943): Lamarr and Powell took a lighter approach as a matrimonial mismatch: he was a serious astronomer; she was an astrology buff. With the exception of one brief cameo, Powell had been off the screen for a year and a half, and his waning interest in the MGM production factory was beginning to show.

WHITE CARGO (1942): Hedy Lamarr was Louis B. Mayer's personal discovery, though he claimed to have been unaware of her scandalous nude scenes in the Czech art-house film *Ecstasy* (1932) when he signed her. Unfortunately, he had a hard time coming up with the right star-making vehicles for her. When pictures like this lurid tale of a South Seas sexpot fizzled, Mayer lost interst in her career.

HER HIGHNESS AND THE BELLBOY (1945): Lamarr was pitted against girl-next-door June Allyson in this plodding romance and came up on the losing end. Post-war audiences were tired of exotic sirens and wanted leading ladies more like the wives and girlfriends who had kept the homefires burning. Lamarr ended her MGM contract with this film. She would make only eleven more films before retiring from the screen in 1957.

White Cargo
(1942) INSERT

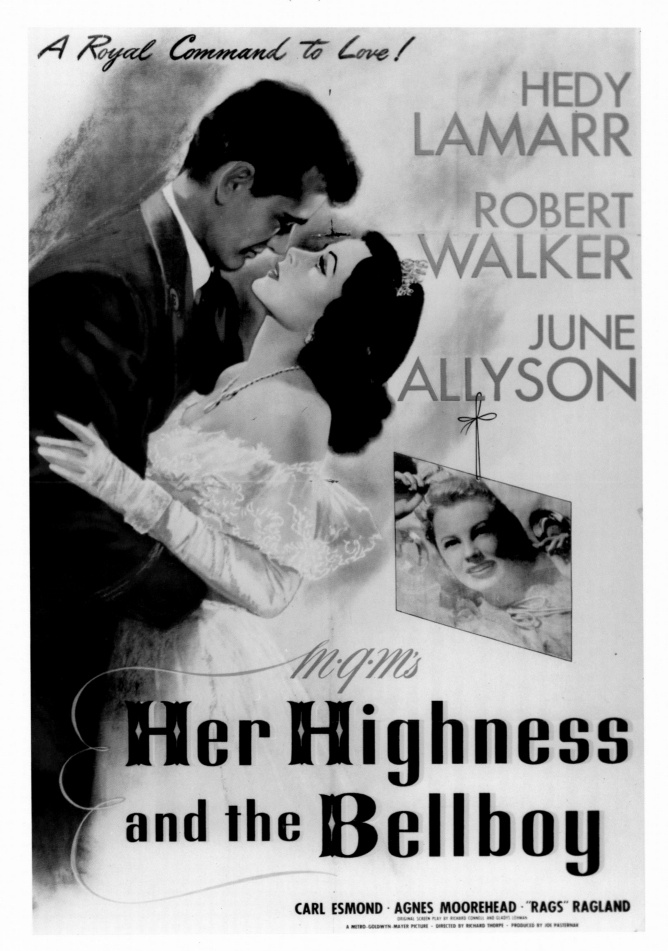

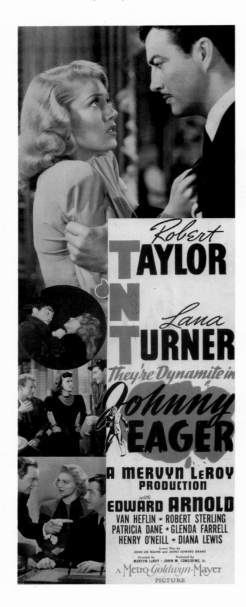

JOHNNY EAGER (1942): Lana Turner's star had been rising since she arrived at MGM in 1938. One of the films that helped make her the studio's new blonde bombshell was this glossy gangster picture, which teamed her with the equally photogenic Robert Taylor, giving the publicity department a chance to herald the team as "T'N'T."

SOMEWHERE I'LL FIND YOU (1942): Turner was showcased opposite all of MGM's top male stars, doing particularly well with Clark Gable in *Honky Tonk* (1941) and this film. Shooting was halted for two weeks when Gable's wife, Carole Lombard, was killed in a plane crash on her way home from a war bond tour.

SLIGHTLY DANGEROUS (1943): The sultry blonde went comic, to great popular success, as a small-town girl who puts on an act to break into high society. The same year this light-hearted film came out, Turner gave birth to daughter Cheryl Crane, whose tormented childhood would be documented in the autobiography *Detour*.

WHAT A FIGURE SHE WAS
BEHIND A SODA COUNTER !
BUT THE SATINS AND
SABLES BROUGHT OUT
THE BEST IN HER !

LANA
Turner
ROBERT
YOUNG
IN

SLIGHTLY
DANGEROUS

with WALTER BRENNAN

DAME MAY WHITTY   EUGENE PALLETTE   ALAN MOWBRAY

SCREEN PLAY BY CHARLES LEDERER AND GEORGE OPPENHEIMER   Directed by WESLEY RUGGLES   Produced by PANDRO S. BERMAN   A Metro-Goldwyn-Mayer PICTURE
STORY BY IAN McLELLAN HUNTER AND AILEEN HAMILTON

135

MARRIAGE IS A PRIVATE AFFAIR (1944): With most of MGM's top male stars fighting World War II, Turner proved she could carry films on her own. It helped that the studio capitalized on the publicity surrounding her daughter's birth to cast her as a spoiled newlywed adjusting to married life and motherhood.

THE POSTMAN ALWAYS RINGS TWICE (1946): It took twelve years for MGM to come up with a film version of James M. Cain's sultry novel that would satisfy the censors. By that time, Turner had developed enough as star and actress to help carry this steamy tale of an adulterous wife who gets her lover (John Garfield) to murder her husband (Cecil Kellaway). Her white-clad vixen made her the hottest sex symbol of the forties.

The Postman Always Rings Twice
(1946) ONE SHEET

The Philadelphia Story

(1940) ONE SHEET
ILLUSTRATOR: ARMANDO SEGUSO

THE PHILADELPHIA STORY (1940):
After leaving Hollywood in disgrace
in 1938, Katharine Hepburn
returned as one of the brightest addi-
tions to the MGM star lineup with
this adaptation of her stage hit, written by Philip Barry. It helped that she
had bought the film rights herself
and wouldn't sell them without a
contract to star. The film was the
highest-grossing stage adaptation in
MGM's history.

WOMAN OF THE YEAR (1942): Hepburn had wanted Spencer Tracy to
co-star in *The Philadelphia Story*, but
he wasn't available at the time. Then,
she discovered the script for this tale
of a sophisticated political columnist
wooed and wed by a rough-hewn
sportswriter. The two were perfect
together, launching an on-screen
team and offscreen romance that
would last for a quarter of a century.

WITHOUT LOVE (1945): Hepburn's
contract allowed her to return to the
stage, which is where she developed
this Philip Barry story about a marriage of convenience during
Washington's World War II housing
shortage. The film was far from her
best teaming with Tracy, but provided juicy supporting roles for Lucille
Ball and Keenan Wynn.

ADAM'S RIB (1949): Tracy and Hepburn finished the forties with one of
their best films. This tale of dueling
husband-and-wife lawyers, slickly
directed by George Cukor, pointed
the way to a new decade, using
laughter to deal with some painful
sexual and social issues.

Woman of the Year

(1942) ONE SHEET

Without Love

(1945) ONE SHEET

138

The Fifties

OUIS B. MAYER AND DORE SCHARY seemed to be pulling MGM in two different directions. The latter brought the new realism to MGM with films like *The Asphalt Jungle*. The former continued to bank on escapism, scoring a big hit of his own with *Show Boat*. ✳ By 1951 they had reached an impasse and could no longer communicate. Realizing that Schary had the backing of Nicholas Schenck, president of Loew's, Inc., the parent company, Mayer resigned. His attempts to purchase Warner Bros. and RKO were unsuccessful. He even tried to mount a stockholder's revolt back at MGM, but to no avail. ✳ The MGM Schary took over was, like the other Hollywood studios, a crumbling giant at the mercy of changing times. The growing popularity of television had cut significantly into movie attendance. In 1948 the Supreme Court forced the studios to sell their theater chains, thus robbing them of their guaranteed market (MGM would hold out against the antitrust action until 1959). And the stars were eschewing long-term studio contracts in favor of independent deals. Weekly salaries were replaced by profit points; star billing by producer status. ✳ The studio mistakenly declared Clark Gable washed up, only to watch the King rise to even greater heights on the strength of his final MGM films, released after his option was dropped. By the decade's end, almost all of the studio's contract players were gone, with Elizabeth Taylor the most notable and unwilling hold-out. ✳ By that point, however, Schary was long gone. He was fired in 1956, the year MGM posted its first loss ever. There were changes at the top of Loew's, Inc., too, with Schenck retiring in 1955 to be replaced first by Arthur Loew and then, a year later, by Joseph Vogel. ✳ Not that the fifties were one long debacle for the studio. The MGM musical reached its zenith with *Singin' in the Rain*, *The Bandwagon*, and two Oscar-winners for Best Picture, *An American in Paris* and *Gigi*. Under Schary, the studio produced hard-hitting dramas like *The Bad and the Beautiful*, *I Want to Live*, and *Blackboard Jungle*. They entered the rock-'n'-roll era by signing Elvis Presley for one of his best films, *Jailhouse Rock*. And the decade ended with MGM's biggest all-time hit and champion Oscar-winner, the 1959 remake of *Ben-Hur*. ✳ But even though *Ben-Hur* was a studio product, it pointed to the end of the old ways. Like many costly spectacles of the decade, it was shot not on Hollywood soundstages but on location (in Rome). The actors and director William Wyler were all independent agents, free to take their box-office luster to other studios. As MGM moved into the sixties, it would make more and more films under these conditions, until the days of studio production became a dim memory of things past.

THE BAD AND THE BEAUTIFUL (1952): Glitz and glamor weren't entirely absent from the studio's dramas, as demonstrated by this behind-the-scenes tale of unscrupulous producer Kirk Douglas' rise and fall. Fans struggled to guess which Hollywood players had inspired this searing look at Hollywood scandal.

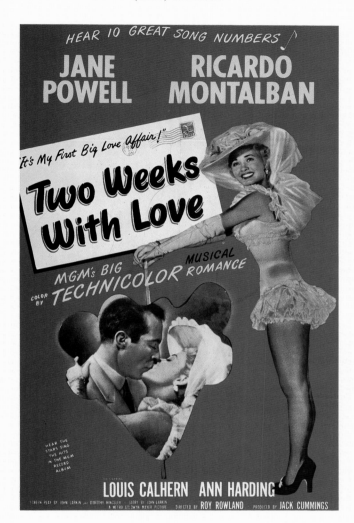

SINGIN' IN THE RAIN (1952): The MGM musical, particularly as produced with taste and intelligence by Arthur Freed, came into its own in the fifties, with Freed producing two Oscar-winners for Best Picture and the film most critics consider the greatest musical of all time. As an added bonus, the picture made a star out of the recently signed Debbie Reynolds.

TWO WEEKS WITH LOVE (1950): Reynolds got her first big break singing "I Wanna Be Loved By You" to Carleton Carpenter in *Three Little Words* (1950). The studio rushed the two into supporting roles in this period musical starring Jane Powell (in her first adult role), and the pair stole the picture with their spirited rendition of "Abba Dabba Honeymoon."

ANNIE GET YOUR GUN (1950): Judy Garland's continuing problems cost her the role of Annie Oakley in this film version of the Irving Berlin stage hit. In her place, MGM borrowed Betty Hutton from Paramount, giving the singing star her best role ever and a big, big hit. Howard Keel made his film debut as rival sharpshooter Frank Butler.

SUMMER STOCK (1950): Garland recovered enough to make her third film with Gene Kelly, but barely made it through the production. Although she needed more rest, the studio pushed her into *Royal Wedding* (1950), then canceled her contract when she didn't show up for work.

AN AMERICAN IN PARIS (1951): Freed won his first Oscar for Best Picture, and Gene Kelly won a special award for his choreography for this elegant tale of an ex-GI who stays in Paris to become a painter. The studio almost cut the climactic eighteen-minute ballet, which turned out to be one of the picture's biggest selling points.

LILI (1953): Audiences everywhere fell in love with French dancer Leslie Caron cast as a French orphan who joins a traveling puppet show in which the characters she loves are performed by a puppeteer she hates. The film would inspire a hit stage musical, *Carnival*, in 1961.

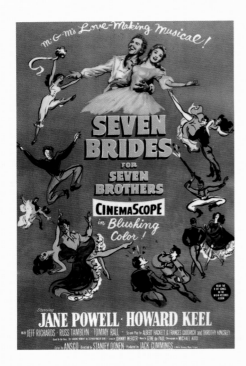

SEVEN BRIDES FOR SEVEN BROTHERS (1954): MGM beat the film version of *Oklahoma!* to the screen by one year with this rousing outdoor musical starring Howard Keel as a hard-living lumberjack and Jane Powell, in her best MGM role, as the wife who tames him and his equally rambunctious brothers.

GIGI (1958): Freed and Minnelli had one last burst of glory with this elegant musical based on Colette's stories about a young Parisian girl raised to be the perfect mistress. The location-shot picture brought Freed his second Oscar for Best Picture and Minnelli his first (and only) for Best Director.

HIGH SOCIETY (1956): Box-office draws Bing Crosby and Frank Sinatra, along with public interest in Grace Kelly's marriage to Prince Ranier of Monaco, helped make this musical version of *The Philadelphia Story* the studio's biggest money-maker of the year. The great Cole Porter score didn't hurt either.

Gigi
(1958) ONE SHEET

A NEW HIGH IN THE MOVIE SKY. M-G-M PRESENTS IN VistaVision AND COLOR
A SOL C. SIEGEL PRODUCTION

Starring

BING CROSBY ★ GRACE KELLY ★ FRANK SINATRA

in the hilarious low-down on high life

High Society

co-starring

CELESTE HOLM · JOHN LUND

LOUIS CALHERN · SIDNEY BLACKMER

and LOUIS ARMSTRONG and His Band

Screen Play by JOHN PATRICK Based on a Play by PHILIP BARRY

Music and Lyrics by COLE PORTER

Color by TECHNICOLOR Directed by CHARLES WALTERS

FORBIDDEN PLANET (1956): MGM took a rare foray into science fiction and did it up royally with this outer space retelling of Shakesepeare's *The Tempest*. Walter Pidgeon, Anne Francis, and a very young, very serious Leslie Nielsen were the nominal stars, but the biggest fan favorite was Robby the Robot.

GREEN MANSIONS (1959): The studio came to a cropper with this classic W. H. Hudson fantasy. Vincente Minnelli had tried to develop a film version for Pier Angeli in 1954 but gave up. Undaunted Mel Ferrer cast his wife, Audrey Hepburn, in one of her biggest flops.

The Asphalt Jungle
(1950) INSERT

THE ASPHALT JUNGLE (1950): John Huston brought a new kind of realism to MGM with this gritty story about the planning, execution and aftermath of a jewel robbery. The film set the style for dozens of caper pictures to come and helped the young Marilyn Monroe in her rise to stardom.

BLACKBOARD JUNGLE (1955): MGM exploited two youthful phenomena—the rise of juvenile delinquency and the popularity of rock 'n' roll—in this well-acted social-problem picture. Among the young actors gaining valuable screen exposure as troubled teens were Sidney Poitier, Vic Morrow, and Jamie Farr.

TORCH SONG (1953): Joan Crawford returned to MGM after a decade to star in a glitzy musical drama of her own. Her performance as a heartless Broadway star who falls for a blind pianist (Michael Wilding) proved that she still had what it takes to carry a picture, from great screen presence to great legs.

Blackboard Jungle
(1955) ONE SHEET

MOGAMBO (1953): Only Gable could top Gable in this remake of his early hit *Red Dust* (1932), with Ava Gardner and Grace Kelly taking over for Jean Harlow and Mary Astor. Foolishly, the studio let Gable's contract lapse after filming was completed. It's box-office success made him a bigger star than ever.

I'LL CRY TOMORROW (1955): Losing out on the chance to play alcoholic singer Lillian Roth helped convince June Allyson to leave MGM, but who could have quarreled with the choice of Susan Hayworth for the role? She even had the backing of Roth herself.

LOVE ME OR LEAVE ME (1955): In the fifties, Hollywood's musical biographies got decidedly grimmer. Ruth Etting's rise to stardom with the help, and hinderance, of gangster Marty "The Gimp" Snyder gave Doris Day a rare dramatic role and allowed James Cagney to turn in one of his best performances.

Mogambo

(1953) ONE SHEET

I'll Cry Tomorrow

(1955) ONE SHEET

You'll Love
DORIS DAY
in M·G·M's
"Love Me or Leave Me"

M·G·M PRESENTS DORIS DAY—JAMES CAGNEY IN "LOVE ME OR LEAVE ME" CO-STARRING CAMERON MITCHELL,
WITH ROBERT KEITH, TOM TULLY. SCREEN PLAY BY DANIEL FUCHS AND ISOBEL LENNART. STORY BY DANIEL FUCHS.
PHOTOGRAPHED IN EASTMAN COLOR. DIRECTED BY CHARLES VIDOR. PRODUCED BY JOE PASTERNAK. IN CINEMASCOPE.

JAILHOUSE ROCK (1957): MGM was wise enough to sign singing sensation Elvis Presley for a series of films, starting with this semi-autobiographical tale of a temperamental singer's rise to fame. Although it was Presley's third film, it was the first to capture his fiery performance style on screen.

BHOWANI JUNCTION (1956): Producers were straying further and further from Hollywood to add authenticity to their stories, as Pandro S. Berman did when he took his crew to Pakistan for this story of a beautiful Eurasian (Ava Gardner) caught up in the revolt against British rule of India.

CAT ON A HOT TIN ROOF (1958): The success of Tennessee Williams' plays on screen marked the birth of a new era of adult films. Elizabeth Taylor and Paul Newman sizzled in roles originally intended for Grace Kelly and James Dean, turning this picture into the studio's biggest money-maker ever.

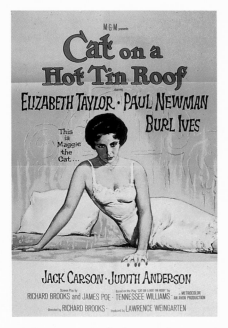

FATHER OF THE BRIDE (1950): Spencer Tracy gave one of his best performances in this tale of wedding-day disasters, but it was publicity over Elizabeth Taylor's first marriage, to hotel heir Nicky Hilton, that helped make this Vincente Minnelli film MGM's top-grossing comedy to date.

PAT AND MIKE (1952): Tracy and his favorite co-star, Katharine Hepburn, had their best film together—and their last at MGM as a team—with this sports comedy built around the leading lady's own athleticism. George Cukor directed gracefully from a script by husband-and-wife team Garson Kanin and Ruth Gordon.

FOREVER DARLING (1956): "If you can't beat 'em, join 'em," was the spirit behind MGM's signing of television superstars Lucille Ball and Desi Arnaz for two romantic comedies. The first, *The Long, Long Trailer* (1954), beat out *Father of the Bride* as the studio's highest-grossing comedy. The second was a surprise flop.

DESIGNING WOMAN (1957): More fortuitous was the teaming of Gregory Peck and Lauren Bacall for this sophisticated tale of a sportswriter and fashion designer who marry in haste and repent until they realize they really are meant for each other.

SCARAMOUCHE (1952): Stewart Granger appeared in another of his swashbuckling roles, this one originally played by Ramon Novarro, as a young man masquerading as an actor to avenge his father's death. At the climax, he and Mel Ferrer faced off for one of the screen's great swordfights.

Scaramouche
(1952) ONE SHEET

THE PRODIGAL (1955): The word "epic" describes both the production values and the stupidity of this classic stinker, with Lana Turner as the pagan priestess who seduces the prodigal son (Edmund Purdom). Films like this helped convince Turner to leave the studio that had made her a star.

RAINTREE COUNTY (1957): Dore Schary hoped to create his own *Gone With the Wind* with this adaptation of Ross Lockridge's novel, but by the time the costly production was finished, so was Schary's career at the studio. During shooting, Montgomery Clift had the auto accident that would destroy his looks and his career.

BEN-HUR (1959): This multimillion dollar production took years to get to the screen, with the stress ultimately taking the life of producer Sam Zimbalist, but brought the studio over $80 million in worldwide rentals and set an all-time record by winning eleven Oscars. Times were changing in Hollywood, and *Ben-Hur* would soon be regarded as the last big hit of the studio era.

The Sixties

"TURBULENT" WAS THE WORD FOR MGM in the sixties as the studio moved uneasily through a world of increasingly independent production and continued declines at the box office. The studio changed management three times and ownership twice. With growing production costs, a single film could spell the difference between profit and loss for an entire year. ✳ MGM continued to show profits for the first two years of the sixties, thanks largely to the continuing success of *Ben-Hur*. But its production schedule had fallen off tremendously, with only twelve features produced by MGM in 1960 and another seven picked up from other companies. Increasingly, MGM would turn to independent producers and international productions for its yearly slate of releases. ✳ The year 1960 marked the departure of MGM's last great contract star. After completing *Butterfield 8*, for which she won her first Oscar, Elizabeth Taylor went off to England and then to Rome to film the disastrous *Cleopatra* for 20th Century-Fox. ✳ As location shooting became the norm and hyphenates ("producer-director," "producer-star," and even "producer-writer") began calling the shots, studios like MGM found it increasingly difficult to control production costs. ✳ In some cases, the new freedom awarded to filmmakers paid off. David Lean spent a fortune on *Dr. Zhivago* but turned in one of the top money-makers of the year. But costs on MGM's remake of *Mutiny on the Bounty* went madly out of control, rising to $19 million and contributing to the studio's record loss of $17.5 million in 1963. ✳ Another trend during the sixties was the relaxation of censorship. With the influx of European films, including many featuring such international sex goddesses as Sophia Loren and Brigitte Bardot, Hollywood had to change its ways fast in order to compete. MGM did its bit with 1962's *Lolita*, a comic look at sexual perversion, In 1968 the Production Code was finally abolishedand replaced by a ratings system that governed not what went on screen but who could get into the theater to see it. ✳ By the late sixties, Americans no longer shared common values, as sweeping social changes were leading to a fragmented audience that would continue to splinter in the seventies as generation and gender gaps widened. ✳ By the close of the decade, MGM once more pointed to the future with Stanley Kubrick's *2001: A Space Odyssey*. Although studio executives predicted disaster, the movie drew record crowds, demonstrating the arrival of a new, younger audience less interested in the solid, craftsmanlike storytelling of the past than in the total sensual experience of moviegoing. With the birth of the star child at *2001*'s climax, the MGM of the golden years was officially dead.

LOLITA (1962): An independent production built around a previously forbidden subject, this adaptation of Vladimir Nabokov's scandalous bestseller pointed to the changes that would spell the end of the old Hollywood—and the old MGM—and lead to an uncertain new world in moviemaking.

Butterfield 8
(1960) ONE SHEET

Bachelor in Paradise
(1961) ONE SHEET

BELLS ARE RINGING (1960): The box-office failure of this sophisticated adaptation of Judy Holliday's biggest stage hit marked the end of the MGM musical as nurtured by producer Arthur Freed, who would produce only one more film, a drama, before retiring from MGM.

BUTTERFIELD 8 (1960): Elizabeth Taylor only agreed to star in this adaptation of John O'Hara's novella to finish off her contract at MGM and get on with her career. Although she hated the film, it won her her first Oscar, largely because she was near death from pneumonia during the balloting.

BACHELOR IN PARADISE (1961): This scintillating sex comedy made better use of the screen's new freedom. Lana Turner returned to MGM as a real estate agent involved with a researcher (Bob Hope, in his first MGM film) studying married couples in suburbia.

Sweet Bird of Youth
(1962) ONE SHEET

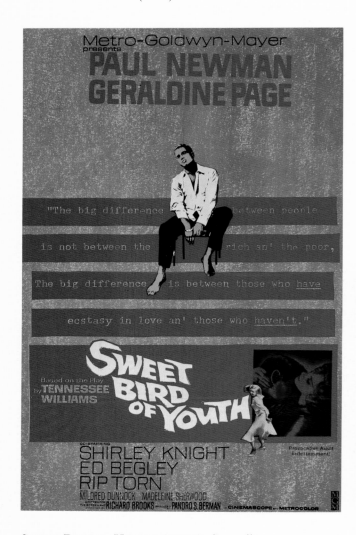

Murder She Said
(1962) ONE SHEET

SWEET BIRD OF YOUTH (1962): Sexuality ran rampant in this Tennessee Williams adaptation, with an electrifying Paul Newman playing a young hustler kept by fading film star Geraldine Page. Writer-director Richard Brooks, who had worked on *Cat On a Hot Tin Roof,* helped turn this into a big winner.

MURDER SHE SAID (1962): MGM's British studio produced a series of hits when Margaret Rutherford starred as Agatha Christie's elderly sleuth Miss Marple in this and three subsequent films. Although the pictures made Rutherford an international star, MGM publicized the first one with shots of the sexy blonde whose murder she solves.

MUTINY ON THE BOUNTY (1962): MGM's taste for production on a grand scale almost bankrupted the studio when this remake of the 1935 classic came in at a cost of $19 million. The production lost one director, Carol Reed, and ended the career of another, veteran Lewis Milestone.

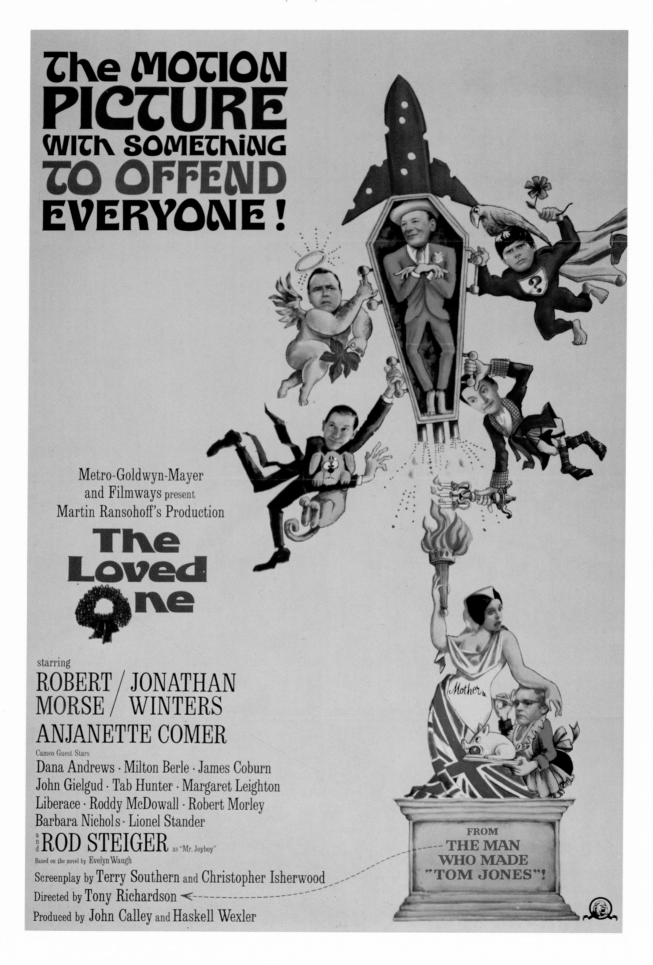

THE LOVED ONE (1965): MGM tried to keep up with changing times by signing the Oscar-winning director of *Tom Jones* (1963), Tony Richardson, for a supposedly with-it adaptation of Evelyn Waugh's satire of the American funeral industry. Despite some strong scenes, the picture as a whole was shunned by critics and audiences alike.

THE V.I.P.s (1963): Elizabeth Taylor returned to MGM with new love Richard Burton to lend box-office luster to this old-fashioned soap opera set in London's Heathrow Airport. For all the headlines about the stars, the picture belonged to two supporting players, Oscar-winner Margaret Rutherford and the young Maggie Smith.

DOCTOR ZHIVAGO (1965): More profitable was David Lean's epic adaptation of Boris Pasternak's novel. Studio executives were horrified by Lean's lengthy shooting schedule and lavish spending, but delighted at the picture's $100 million in worldwide rentals.

The V.I.P.s

(1963) ONE SHEET

Doctor Zhivago

(1965) ONE SHEET

FAR FROM THE MADDING CROWD (1967): To recapture the magic of *Doctor Zhivago*, MGM cast the film's star, Julie Christie, in another epic romance, this time adapted from Thomas Hardy's novel. Despite praise for individual production elements—including Nicholas Roeg's cinematography and Richard Rodney Bennett's score—the film as a whole did not come together.

MADE IN PARIS (1965): MGM veteran Joe Pasternak cast rising star Ann-Margret as a young fashion designer transformed by her first trip to Paris, the kind of glamorous role that had made stars out of Lana Turner and many another studio star. The results, however, were far from impressive.

Far From the Madding Crowd
(1967) ONE SHEET

VIVA LAS VEGAS (1964): Elvis Presley continued as one of MGM's most profitable contract stars long after the rest of the studio's talent pool had departed. His best-remembered film of the decade was this spirited musical with Ann-Margret, the only co-star ever to match his animal magnetism.

GIRL HAPPY (1965): Less of a career peak, though no less popular with the fans, was Presley's role as a singer hired to keep an eye on a gangster's daughter (Shelley Fabares). Even the King's staunchest fans couldn't miss the incongruous sight of mountains in the background of this Florida-set tale.

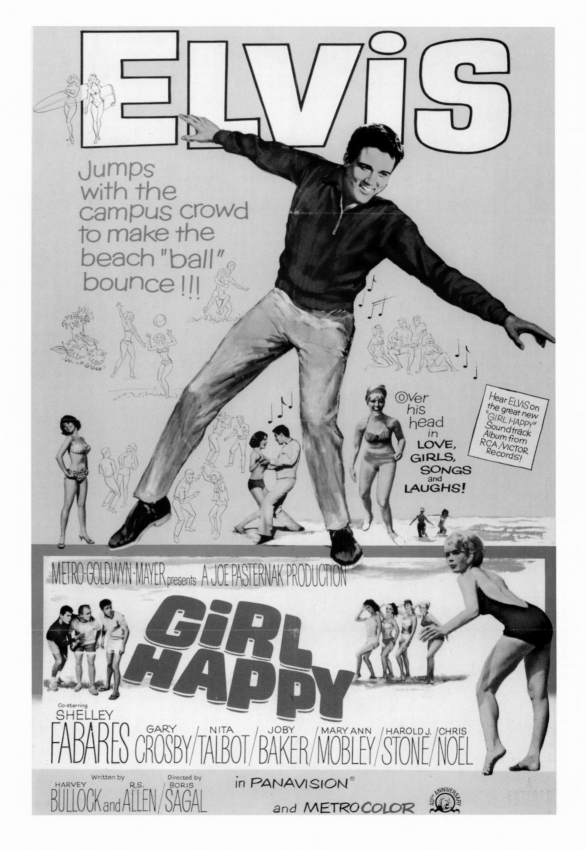

The Dirty Dozen

(1967) ONE SHEET

THE DIRTY DOZEN (1967): As American life grew more violent in the sixties, filmmakers, freed from most censors' restraints, followed suit. Robert Aldrich's hard-hitting wartime adventure spawned a horde of imitators, but also triggered protests against on-screen brutality. One critic even suggested that it had helped cause the Detroit race riots.

POINT BLANK (1967): This early film from British director John Boorman was criticized for the heavy violence in its tale of a criminal (Lee Marvin) out for revenge on the wife and partner who betrayed him. Later critics, however, have hailed it as one of the great films of the sixties.

THE FASTEST GUITAR ALIVE (1968): MGM was hardly the only studio out to capitalize on the growing popularity of pop music, but it proved to have the strangest ideas about how to do so. In his only film, Roy Orbison starred as a Confederate spy who keeps a rifle hidden you know where.

DIRTY WEEKEND (1966): Originally titled *Weekend, Italian Style;* this continental comedy from producer Carlo Ponti tried to capitalize on the popularity of Marcello Mastroianni's other sex comedies of the sixties, including *Divorce, Italian Style;* and *Marriage, Italian Style.*

TWO WOMEN (1961): Film truly became an international language in the sixties, with studios like MGM picking up U.S. distribution rights to an ever-growing slate of European features. In this case, the investment paid off, with Sophia Loren becoming the only performer to win an Oscar for a foreign-language film.

2001: A SPACE ODYSSEY (1968): Stanley Kubrick's science-fiction epic about the dawn of a new age for humanity also signaled Hollywood's ultimate transition to a new age of filmmaking. Studio executives fought in vein to rein in the independent producer-director, only to see this film become a major hit in defiance of all conventional storytelling techniques. The old ways of moviemaking were gone for good as MGM and other studios struggled to attract the young audience that flocked to see this enigmatic tale with its psychedelic space-ride finale.

Two Women

(1961) ONE SHEET

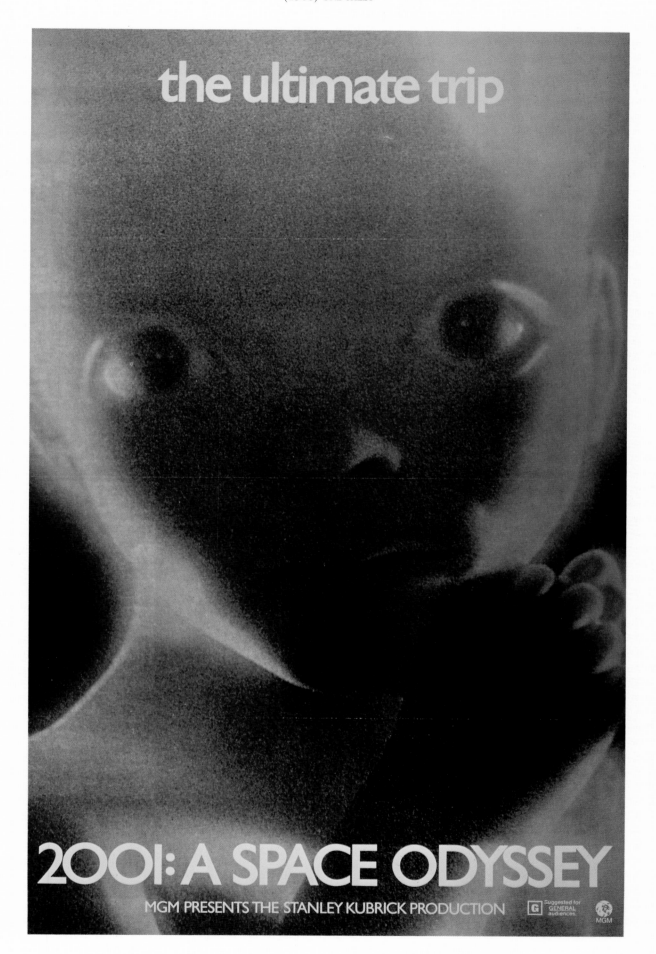

Index

References to artwork are printed in *italics*. Numbers in **boldface** type refer to the captions.

Acknowledgments

POSTERS COURTESY OF

Turner Entertainment Company, Entertainment Film and Tape Services still collection

Butterfield and Butterfield, thanks to Glenn Brown-Entertainment and Memorabilia

Woolsey Ackerman

Gary Bell

John Fricke

Gus Marrone

Dennis Millay

Patrick Miller

Rick Skye

Willard Carroll

Marvin Paige's Motion Picture and Television Research Archive

Thanks to staff of Academy of Motion Picture Arts and Sciences,
Margaret Herrick Library, and Producers Photo Lab, Hollywood, California.

About the Author:

FRANK MILLER first discovered the world of the silver screen at age six when an aunt took him to one of the last theatrical reissues of *The Wizard of Oz*. On his own personal trip down the yellow brick road, he acquired a few more favorite films—*Citizen Kane, The Thing (From Another World), The Lady Eve, In a Lonely Place, The Bandwagon*—and a Ph.D. in dramatic literature and criticism from Ohio State University.

Miller has hosted a short-lived radio show, where he reviewed film and television for WUTS-FM in Tennessee, and has credits for writing the television retrospectives "Andy's Silver Anniversary Special with Don Knotts" and "America's Lawyer: Perry Mason with Barbara Hale." As a theater professional, he has directed productions of *Henry V, Fallen Angels, Lend Me a Tenor*, and most recently, *The Hostage*. He is also a respected acting teacher.

Dr. Miller is the author of *Casablanca: As Time Goes By* and *Censored Hollywood*. He lives near Atlanta.